NEIGHBORHOOD POLITICS

Residential Community Associations in American Governance

Robert Jay Dilger

NEW YORK UNIVERSITY PRESS
New York and London

NEW YORK UNIVERSITY PRESS
New York and London

Library of Congress Cataloging-in-Publication Data
Dilger, Robert Jay, 1954–
Neighborhood politics : residential community associations in American governance / Robert Jay Dilger.
p. cm.
Includes bibliographical references and index.
ISBN 0-8147-1847-7 (alk. paper)
1. Homeowners' associations—United States. 2. Neighborhood government—United States. 3. Privatization—United States.
I. Title.
HD7287.82.U6D55 1992
323'.042'0973—dc20 92-12804
CIP

New York University Press books are printed on acid-free paper, and their binding materials are chosen for strength and durability.

Manufactured in the United States of America

c 10 9 8 7 6 5 4 3 2 1

To Gloria, Anne, and Alex

Contents

Acknowledgments ix

1 Introduction 1

2 RCAs' Characteristics, Functions, and Issues of Concern 12

3 RCAs' Historical Development 41

4 The Privatization of Public Services: The Theoretical Arguments 61

5 RCAs and the Privatization Movement 87

6 RCAs and Local Government Interaction 104

7 RCAs and Civic Virtue 131

8 Conclusions 145

References 163

Index 173

Acknowledgments

This book would not have been possible without the assistance and support of many people. I owe a special debt of gratitude to my neighbors who served with me on the board of directors of the Orange Park Homeowners' Association in Redlands, California, especially Ginger and Paul Huddleston, Tina and Jim Leeds, Ernie Sanchez, Mary Kay Carrillo, Robert Morris, Jack and Janet Hartin, Arjun Koil, Ken Clifford, Gordon Campbell and Bill Jones. Their collective efforts to protect the neighborhood's property values and aesthetics from urban encroachment inspired me to write this book.

I would also like to thank Douglas Kleine, Director of Research at the Community Associations Institute, for providing me access to the Institute's membership list. The list was used to generate the sample for a nationwide survey of residential community associations' board members. It would have been impossible to conduct the survey without his assistance. I would also like to express my gratitude to Debra Dean, research associate with the U.S. Advisory Commission on Intergovernmental Relations, for reviewing the survey and making several valuable suggestions for improving it and to the John and Dora Haynes Research Foundation and the American Political Science Association for providing me financial assistance used to underwrite the costs of conducting the survey.

I owe a special thank you to the following undergraduate students at the University of Redlands who assisted me in collecting, coding, and entering the survey's data into the computer for analysis: Wes Burns, Michael Caspino, Debra Dykes, Douglas Evans, Patrick Fry, Brian Kohn, Michael McFarlane, Christine Opitz, Kathryn Sarna, Robin Spriggs, Christine Stanton, Erin Stehle, Robin Tittle, and Thomas Walker. Also, Randy Moffett, my graduate research assistant at West Virginia University, deserves a special thank you for making all those trips to the library on my behalf and for reading and commenting on various chapters in the book.

I would also like to express my appreciation to the Carl Vinson Institute of Government at the University of Georgia for allowing me to use some of the material that originally appeared in my article, "Residential Community Associations: Issues, Impacts, and Relevance for Local Government," *State and Local Government Review,* 23:1 (Winter 1991): 17–23.

I am also indebted to several of my colleagues at West Virginia University, especially Richard Brisbin, Susan Hunter, Kevin Leyden, and Christopher Mooney, who were kind enough to read and comment on various chapters in this book. Their suggestions have enabled me to present the arguments in a more clear and precise manner. Of course, I assume full responsibility for any errors of fact, omission, or misinterpretation.

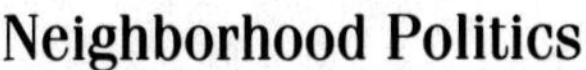

1

Introduction

There are over 150,000 residential community associations (RCAs) in the United States. They are nonprofit corporations that are created by real estate developers with the approval of local government officials. They provide homeowners in master-planned, single-family housing developments, condominium developments, and cooperatives with a governing mechanism to manage commonly owned property in their neighborhood, such as streets, parking lots, park land, and recreational facilities. They also supply various services in the neighborhood, such as street maintenance, trash collection, snow removal, and water and sewer services. They also determine and collect assessment fees to pay for these facilities and services. Finally, they create and enforce commonly held covenants, rules, and regulations (CC&Rs) that regulate the behavior of the residents in the housing development. The CC&Rs can, among other things, determine whether and under what conditions homeowners can own a dog or a cat, build an addition onto their home, have a television antenna on their roofs or park their car in front of their home or in front of a neighbor's home.

RCAs result from the interactions among home buyers looking for alternatives to the traditional residential subdivision that typically does not have commonly owned properties or amenities, real estate developers eager to build and sell homes to this segment of the home-buying market, and local government officials seeking to provide their constituents with affordable housing while, at the same time, preserving their community's aesthetics and fiscal well-being [Advisory Commission on Intergovernmental Relations (hereafter ACIR) ACIR 1989]. What makes RCAs unique and particularly interesting is that they are private organizations that strain the distinction that normally exists between public and private associations. Although RCAs use existing business forms of association to hold and exercise common law servitudes, they also have many attributes traditionally associated with the public sector. For example, to encourage local government officials to approve their site plans and to issue building permits for their development, real estate developers often have the RCA offer many services that are normally provided by local governments, such as street maintenance, recreational facilities and parks, enforcement of parking regulations, trash collection, and snow removal. By supplying these services, the RCA reduces the local government's operating expenses, particularly for infrastructure. Moreover, like the public sector, RCAs have the authority to "tax" their residents for these services through regular and special assessments. In addition, they have the authority, similar to local policing powers, to enforce the community's behavioral standards and punish offenders by placing a lien upon their property. Also, like the public sector, they hold periodic elections based on the republican principle of representative democracy to determine who will make decisions on behalf of the neighborhood. The RCA's board of directors and its president act like city councils and mayors as they adopt rules and regulations regarding the use of common areas, the provision of services, and the enforcement or modification of the CC&Rs. They also have rules, like governments, that determine such issues as suffrage rights, what constitutes a quorum, whether proxy voting is allowed, and how often general meetings of the entire membership are to occur. As a result, in many ways, RCAs have not only assumed some of the functions of local governments but have also assumed a part of the local political process, shifting it into a private framework. As one study has suggested, RCAs are technically private contractual arrangements among their members but function as a de facto government (Tarlock 1989). Other studies have described them as minigovernments and as private governments (Dowden 1986; Barton and Silverman 1989).

Traditionally, American law has drawn a distinction between public and private associations to decide how power should be allocated between the state and the individual. The constitutional and other doctrines that courts have enforced to protect individuals from the abuse of state power are generally not viewed as being necessary to protect individuals who consent voluntarily to a private association. For example, the constitutional limitations and protection embodied in the First and Fourteenth Amendments to the U.S. Constitution (free speech, due process of law, equal protection of the laws, etc.) apply only to governmental actions. They do not affect private conduct, no matter how discriminatory or wrongful (Rosenberry 1989). However, RCAs strain the distinction between public and private action (Tarlock 1989). They not only have "public" functions but, unlike neighborhood civic associations and other organized interest groups that exist in the private sector and engage in political or what may be termed "public" activities, the decision to join a RCA is not voluntary. Membership in the RCA is automatic and compulsory for everyone who purchases a property interest in the development (Isaacson and Segal 1981; ACIR 1989). Residents in RCA-governed neighborhoods are not given the option to choose to associate themselves with their neighbors or to remain separate. As a result, the courts have had a very difficult time determining whether constitutional controls over state actions apply to RCAs and their board of directors. However, they have had little difficulty in determining that RCA actions, like those of other corporations, must not exceed the scope of its authority as defined by the laws of the state where it is located; that the board of directors must abide by the business-judgment rule when making its decisions (they must act in good faith and use such care as an ordinarily prudent person in a like position should use under similar circumstances), and that board members have a fiduciary duty to the association not to enhance their own position at the expense of the association (Rosenberry 1985, 1989).

Until fairly recently, the number of RCAs in the United States was relatively small and their impact on American society and local governance fairly limited. In 1960 there were fewer than 1,000 RCAs in the United States and most were homeowners' associations located in relatively exclusive master-planned, single-family home housing developments (often referred to as planned unit developments). At the time, the stereotypical view of RCAs brought up images of mansions with meticulously manicured lawns and gardens and of gray-haired executives and their spouses lounging by the pool and sipping martinis. But during the 1960s the number of RCAs began to increase as planned unit developments (PUDs) and condominiums began to gain greater acceptance among American home buyers of more modest means. Although most of the PUDs were still targeted at middle- and upper-income home buyers, the increasing popularity of condominiums that were designed to meet the economic and service needs of the elderly and first-time home buyers began to erode the stereotypical view that RCAs were something associated only with the rich.

By 1980, the number of RCAs had increased to 35,000. However, despite their increasing numbers, RCAs, for the most part, continued to be of interest only to those involved in the real estate industry and to local government officials who were responsible, through their zoning authority, for approving PUDs, condominium developments, and cooperatives. The typical issues discussed at local government meetings at that time included questions concerning how PUDs, condominiums, and cooperatives could meet the housing needs of particular segments of the housing market, particularly those with modest incomes, and whether it was in the public's interest to approve developer requests for zoning variances concerning lot sizes, street widths, and other construction standards in exchange for the provision of amenities such as open spaces, recreational facilities, and privately owned and maintained streets. In addition, local government officials were particularly interested in determining if RCA-governed neighborhoods could save them money by providing the neighborhood's residents with recreational facilities and by assuming some of the neighborhood's infrastructure costs (for its streets, street lighting, water and sewer lines, parking lots, etc.). Relatively little attention was paid to the impacts RCAs might have on the delivery of services that are typically provided by the public sector. Nor was there any consideration given to the prospect that RCAs might act like lobbying organizations and in their attempts to alter local government decisions might change the way local governments reach their decisions. There was also little debate concerning how RCAs might affect the political socialization and political orientation of its members or whether it was important for RCAs' governing procedures to reflect democratic values or to adhere to the principles embodied in the First and Fourteenth Amendments to the U.S. Constitution.

During the 1980s, PUDs and especially condominiums became increasingly popular with a home-buying public that valued the cost savings brought about by common ownership of recreational facilities and other amenities, and the increased amount of leisure time promised by having their RCA assume many of their time consuming chores such as lawn care. As PUDs and condominium sales soared, so did the number of RCAs. By the end of the decade, there were more than 130,000 RCAs operating in the United States and more than 30 million Americans were subject to RCA governance. The number of RCAs in the United States is currently increasing by approximately 9,500 annually and is expected to reach 225,000 by the year 2000 (Community Associations Institute 1988; Winokur 1989a). Assuming that the RCAs created in the next few years are approximately the same size as those already in existence (approximately 230 residents per RCA), the number of Americans subject to RCA governance will grow by approximately 2.1 million annually and will exceed 50 million by the year 2000.

Although the number of RCAs continues to climb and the number of people subject to their governance continues to skyrocket, other than journal articles written by attorneys and legal scholars that attempt to grapple with the legal complexities involving RCA litigation, primarily involving the authority of board of directors to enforce the neighborhood's CC&Rs, RCAs have not generated a great deal of study or interest from the academic community. However, RCAs deserve much greater attention because they are important actors in our intergovernmental system of governance. Their importance was brought to the attention of this author in a rather unusual setting: a public hearing sponsored by the Redlands Unified School District, located in Redlands, California. Over 200 people had gathered to learn about and discuss the location of a proposed second high school for the city of Redlands. The local newspaper had indicated that the school board had narrowed its choice for the location of the new high school to five potential sites. As one might expect, most of the people at the hearing lived near a proposed site and were convinced that their property values and quality of life would be adversely affected if the school board decided to build the new high school near their homes. Not surprisingly, twenty-nine of the thirty people who spoke at the public hearing asked the school board not to build the high school near their homes. They were convinced that it would increase traffic, litter, loitering, and noise in and around their neighborhoods. A few homeowners also indicated that they were afraid that if the new high school was built near their homes that drug dealers and other "criminal types" would be attracted to their neighborhoods.

Only one of the thirty speakers at the public hearing did not object to any of the school board's proposed sites. He lived near the existing high school. In a rising and heated voice, he announced that he had not planned to speak at the meeting but was upset that everyone seemed to think that all high school kids were either drug addicts or trouble-makers. He lectured the audience, letting them know that most high school students are nice people and that living near a high school was not a total disaster.

Many of the comments at this school board hearing were typical of what one would expect to find at a local government public hearing. What was surprising was that all but one of the thirty speakers, the one home owner who lived near the existing high school, prefaced their remarks by identifying themselves as either an officer or as a member of a residential community association. It was obvious that several RCAs located near the proposed sites had "packed" the meeting room with members and had spent considerable time selecting speakers and determining exactly what they would say. Several associations asked the school board to let their members come forward as a group and speak in a particular sequence, with each speaker citing a different reason why building the new high school near their neighborhood would be a bad idea.

Some of the speakers read from prepared texts, citing local zoning ordinances and statistics culled from the draft environmental review document that had been prepared for the school board. All in all, the speakers did an excellent job defending their property values and their neighborhood's aesthetics. Apparently, the local school board was impressed as well. Redlands' school superintendent subsequently announced that the new high school would be built in a location where there were few existing homes (or RCAs to contend with) (Holland 1989).

The actions of Redlands' RCAs suggested that RCAs may be an overlooked but influential lobbying force at the local government level. A computer search of the social science indexes revealed that very little academic research had been conducted on RCAs' interaction with local government officials. However, a 1986 survey of RCA board of directors' presidents located in California sponsored by the California Department of Real Estate and another nationwide survey of RCA board of directors' members conducted in 1988 by the U.S. Advisory Commission on Intergovernmental Relations suggested that what had occurred at the Redlands school board's public hearing was not an isolated incident. Both surveys indicated that RCAs do not hesitate to let their local officials know their views when police protection is perceived to be wanting, or when local development, traffic patterns, or zoning decisions are perceived to jeopardize their quality of life or property values (Barton and Silverman 1987a; ACIR 1988). Moreover, newspaper accounts of RCAs' activities across the country also suggested that RCA board of directors' members, especially in urban areas, are regular participants at city council and county supervisors' meetings. Complaining about urban encroachment and undesirable development in surrounding areas, such as the placement of airports and landfills, RCAs are in the vanguard of the NIMBY (Not In My Back Yard) movement across America (Vesey 1983; Marchese 1987; Hornblower 1988).

Although RCAs have received fairly widespread newspaper coverage, the leading textbooks on state and local government and intergovernmental relations generally do not mention them. Because they are private organizations, RCAs are not recognized as a form of government or as being participants in the intergovernmental system of governance. But as a recent report of the U.S. Advisory Commission on Intergovernmental Relations (ACIR) states, although RCAs are not governments per se, they deserve greater attention because they display many characteristics of traditionally defined local governments and in performing their functions they do affect state and local governments (Hawkins 1989).

Other Reasons to Study RCAs

Discussions of public policy in the United States frequently center on the "what should we do?" question. For example, we often ask "Should we guarantee the poor a minimum income or provide assistance only to those who 'deserve' assistance?"; "Should we target our resources to those communities in greatest need or provide individuals the means to escape from these communities?"; or "Should we target our resources to those needing remedial education or to those who are intellectually gifted?"

It is understandable why elected officials focus on the question of "what should we do," since constituents and lobby organizations ask them regularly to do something on their behalf. However, before we can answer the "what should we do" question we must first ask and answer the "who should decide" question (Henig 1985). Should the strategies employed to care for the poor or the elderly, to deal with urban or rural decline, or to educate the nation's children be determined by state governments, local governments, or the national government? Moreover, should government at any level be involved at all? Should the primary responsibility for dealing with poverty be met by government or by the efforts of charities, churches, and individual families? Can neighbors, cooperating among themselves, do more to prevent crime than government officials (Henig 1985)? If neighbors, organized into residential community associations, can provide public goods and services more effectively and efficiently than government, should they be allowed or encouraged to provide them?

A careful examination of the arguments presented by those who advocate one level of government as opposed to another and by those who advocate an emphasis on the private sector versus those who advocate an emphasis on the public sector is presented in Chapter 4. However, none of these arguments, not even those from the advocates of privatizing governmental services, take into account RCAs' role in providing many services that are typically offered by local governments. Although the privatization literature fails to devote much attention to RCAs' role in providing services, RCAs do supply many goods and services to their neighborhoods that would otherwise be provided by their local government, including but not limited to trash collection, park and recreational facilities, street repair and lighting, water and sewer services, and snow removal. As a recent report by the U.S. Advisory Commission on Intergovernmental Relations indicated, public finance statistics do not include estimates of how much money RCAs spend on otherwise public services, or of the precise extent to which RCA members subsidize the public services of others in their communities. However, in all probability, RCAs account for the most significant privatization of public services in recent times (ACIR 1989). As a result, RCAs serve as an excellent laboratory for testing the desirability of load shedding local government services. Moreover, the examination of RCAs and their impact on the provision of "public" goods and services may offer some guidance in answering one of the most fundamental and important questions concerning our intergovernmental system of governance: "who should decide?" RCAs also deserve greater attention because they are a sociological phenomenon of great importance. As mentioned previously, more than 30 million Americans are currently members of an RCA and that number is expected to increase dramatically over the next decade. This growth is expected to be particularly strong on the east and west coasts where condominium and homeowners' associations are most prevalent. As participants in their RCA's decisionmaking processes, RCA members are routinely asked to determine collectively what is appropriate behavior for their neighborhood and are asked to grapple with such complex problems as the division of maintenance responsibilities between the association and the individual home owners, the requirement of due process in the enforcement of the association's CC&Rs, the provision of recreational and social services such as day care, and the need to fund reserves for the replacement of roofs, roads, plumbing and other commonly owned property. As one study indicated,

> Community associations have responsibilities both great and small, and are the stage for what is sometimes drama, sometimes soap opera, as thousands of ordinary people try to work together both for their own individual benefit and for the common good of their community (Barton and Silverman 1987a).

For millions of American citizens their RCA is a decisionmaking institution that is as important to them, if not more so, than any of their local government institutions. RCAs provide citizens an arena for resolving conflicts and reaching collective decisions that affect both their own homes and their entire neighborhood. As such, the operation of RCAs and their success or failure will tell us much about ourselves as a people and the quality of life we want and expect in our neighborhoods throughout the United States.

The Book's Goals

The primary goal of this book is to examine RCAs' role in the American intergovernmental system of governance. It identifies the extent and nature of RCA services and operations, documents their development as a housing and land-use planning innovation, analyzes their role in providing services typically associated with local governments, and examines their relationships with local government officials, their impact on local politics, and their implications for American governance and democratic values. It argues that RCAs are important actors in the intergovernmental system and do play an increasingly influential role in local government policymaking. It also argues that economic conditions and consumer preferences suggest that RCAs will continue to play an influential role in American governance well into the future. Finally, it argues that anyone interested in understanding local politics and American governance must be aware of and knowledgeable about RCAs and their activities.

The book's secondary goal is to acknowledge and highlight RCAs' role both as a reflection of and as a determining factor in the making of the American lifestyle. Although Americans continue to value the primacy of individual property rights in the United States, where everyone has a right to do whatever they please with their property, there are many who gladly transfer some of their property rights to their RCA in exchange for the protection it provides against any eccentric or egregious behavior by their neighbors. Although some denigrate RCAs as a convenient and relatively painless mechanism for the rich and the middle class to escape the sometimes harsh realities of urban life without doing anything to improve those realities and others complain that some RCAs do not follow democratic principles when reaching their decisions, provide adequate due-process protection to its members when enforcing the neighborhood's CC&Rs, or possess the technical expertise to provide goods and services in an efficient and effective manner, most RCA members share the view of Albert Riendeau, a resident of Leisure World, one of the largest RCAs in the Washington, D.C., area:

> We've got the greenest grass in the world. Great esprit de corps. We have a saying, "If heaven is any nicer than this, it must be one hell of a place" (Garreau 1987).

2

RCAs' Characteristics, Functions, and Issues of Concern

This chapter provides an overview of residential community associations' (RCAs) characteristics, noting, when necessary, the differences that exist among homeowners' associations, condominium associations, and cooperative associations. It also lists RCAs' four primary functions, gives an overview of their lobbying efforts and impact on local government policymaking, and examines several intergovernmental issues of concern that their existence and activities raise, particularly for local government officials. Finally, it presents both the arguments of those who advocate RCAs' formation and those who view them more critically.

What Are RCAs?

RCAs are private, nonprofit corporations that are established by residential developers with local government approval (Longhini and Mosena 1978). Typically, each RCA begins its history long before any home buyers move into the housing development. In most cases, after a developer takes title to a tract of land and has preliminary plans approved by the local planning commission, he or she will record the subdivision and will use most, if not all, of the following six legal documents to create the RCA: the subdivision or condominium plat, the subdivision or condominium declaration, individual unit deeds, articles of incorporation, bylaws, and the declaration of covenants.

The subdivision or condominium plat describes the location of the common properties and the homes. It is usually prepared by a certified engineer, architect, or land surveyor and is recorded in the local land records. It graphically establishes the development's perimeters and boundaries and the precise location of residences and common areas. The subdivision or condominium declaration defines the common properties, the basis for and the percentage of interest in the common properties, and the voting rights concerning their use, maintenance, and upkeep. It also requires all property owners in the development to be members of the RCA, determines the proportional obligation for assessments, and indicates any land use restrictions. The individual unit deeds assign a percentage of ownership interest in the common properties.

The articles of incorporation establish the RCA as a mutual benefit, nonprofit corporation in accordance to the laws of the jurisdiction where it is located. It usually provides a legal description of the corporation, indicating its name and location. It also lists the RCA's powers and purposes, specifying activities such as the maintenance, preservation, and architectural control of lots and common areas, creates the board of directors, determines membership and voting rights, and lists the procedures for adopting amendments and for dissolving the corporation. Although many RCAs, particularly the larger ones (more than 100 units), are incorporated, most RCAs are not incorporated and rely on the declaration of covenants to specify the RCA's powers, purposes, and procedures.

The bylaws describe the rights and duties of RCA membership. They usually establish the RCA's operating procedures, such as when general membership meetings are to be held (typically annually or biannually) and under what circumstances special meetings may be called, how members are to be notified of meetings, what constitutes a quorum (usually a majority of the property owners), and whether proxy voting is allowed. They also typically include provisions relating to the board of directors, such as determining their number (usually five or seven), whether they will be compensated (usually not, although 40 percent of RCA presidents in a recent nationwide survey indicated that they were reimbursed for out-of-pocket expenses, Dale and McBee 1988), the procedures for nominating and electing board members, how often board meetings are to occur (usually monthly), and how board meetings are to be run. The bylaws also usually include provisions that determine how committees and task forces are to be established, the amount and type of insurance the RCA should secure and maintain, and what fiscal and financial accounting procedures are to be followed.

The declaration of covenants is usually recorded in the land records prior to the sale of any home or lot in the development. It separates RCAs from most other forms of association. It includes most of the information contained in the articles of incorporation, including who becomes a member of the association and how members' voting rights are determined. It also describes any restrictions on the use of lots or residences in the development, such as prohibitions against livestock, pets, or billboards. It typically contains provisions that limit an owner's right to modify or alter property without the consent of the board of directors or an architectural review committee. It also describes any easements required for the maintenance and repair of the common areas and provides the RCA with the authority to charge reasonable user fees, collect assessments, and impose new or modify existing covenants, rules, or regulations subject to the procedures outlined in the bylaws. It also grants the RCA the authority to institute liens and imposes on the owners the personal obligation for paying assessments (Isaacson and Segal 1981; Dowden 1986).

The RCA's articles of incorporation, bylaws, and CC&Rs are subject to the approval of local planning officials, the developer's mortgagee, and, in many instances, are written to conform to guidelines issued by lenders such as the Federal Housing Administration, Veterans Administration, Federal Home Loan Mortgage Corporation, and Federal National Mortgage Association (Urban Land Institute 1964; Jackson 1977; Isaacson and Segal 1981). Lenders are particularly interested in assuring that the RCA has sufficient funds to maintain the common properties since the condition of these properties directly affects the value of the homes in the neighborhood. As a result, they generally require very specific assurances in the CC&Rs that the RCA has the authority to collect reasonable assessments from every property owner in the development, that the obligation to pay assessments runs with the land in perpetuity, that RCAs have in place procedures to deal with delinquent assessments and are given the authority to charge interest on delinquent assessments, that the board of directors have the authority to increase assessments to account for changes in the consumer price index without a vote of the general membership, and that there are procedural mechanisms in place for regular assessment increases that exceed the rate of inflation and for special assessments to deal with unforeseen financial difficulties (Urban Land Institute 1964; Federal Housing Administration 1965; Dowden 1986).

The articles of incorporation, bylaws, and CC&Rs create the RCA, determine its governance procedures, and establish eligibility guidelines for determining who can participate in its decisions. They also establish the initial rules and regulations that affect the residents' behavior in the development, determine the services the RCA will provide, the facilities it will maintain, and the initial assessment fee required for the RCA's expenses. The CC&Rs are binding legal documents that run with the land and are enforceable as a lien against the property. As a result, when someone purchases a home in the development they automatically become a member of the RCA and must abide by the rules and regulations spelled out in its CC&Rs.

When the Homeowners Take Control

When developers create a RCA, they usually designate themselves and/or their business partners and employees as members of the RCA's board of directors. In master-planned, single-family housing developments, the developer then constructs a group of model homes and an improved common property, such as a recreational area, swimming pool, or tennis court. As the developer markets the housing development and continues to build and sell homes, he or she continues to control the RCA until a substantial percentage of the homes in the development are sold. Typically, developers establish a two-part voting classification system that allows them to control the RCA until 75 percent of the homes have been sold. This is accomplished by assigning three votes to each lot owned by the developer and only one vote to each lot sold to the public. In this way, 75 percent of the lots must be sold before the homeowners have the same number of votes as the developer. At that time, the developer typically turns the control of the organization over to the homeowners (Dowden 1986; Miller 1989). A similar process, without the weighted voting system, occurs for condominium associations, with the homeowners taking control of the RCA after a substantial percentage of the condominiums in the development has been sold (usually 75 percent).

Three Basic Types of RCAs

Most RCAs are classified as being one of the following three general association types: condominium associations, homeowners' associations, and cooperatives. Condominium associations (COAs) are typically located in multi-family, multi-story buildings. The homeowners hold title to the interior space of their residences and hold the rest of the property (dividing walls, hallways, stairways, elevators, exterior walls, and land) in common. The association does not own any property, but manages it for the common owners. Homeowners' associations (HOAs) typically consist of detached houses or townhouses with common areas. The homeowners own both the interior and exterior of their residences as well as the land beneath and immediately around them. The association owns and manages common property (such as swimming pools, tennis courts, park land, and streets) on their behalf. Cooperative associations are typically associated with multi-family, high-rise buildings in urban areas. Members of the association do not own any real property. Instead, they acquire a long-term renewable leasehold interest in their residence, plus a share (or proportionate shares) in a corporation that owns the building and grounds (Dowden 1980; Dean 1988). There are relatively few cooperatives in the United States because their members are subject to a blanket mortgage, where each of the homeowners is obligated through their leases to contribute their share to the mortgage's amortization and interest. If economic conditions suddenly worsen and there are a large number of foreclosed and empty units in the cooperative, that blanket mortgage obligation can prove to be prohibitive (Urban Land Institute 1964).

Although these technical differences among the three association types are important to the affected homeowners, for the purposes of this book all three associations will be collectively referred to as RCAs. In a few instances, a distinction among the types will be made when warranted. As Table 2.1 indicates, approximately 61 percent of all RCAs are condominium associations, 35 percent are homeowners' associations, and 4 percent are cooperative or other types of associations.

RCAs also display some structural variety. Some of them are very complex, involving a federation of numerous local associations and one or more larger umbrella associations. For example, The Country Club District in Kansas City encompasses 11,695 homes located in 29 RCAs. Each of those 29 RCAs is a separate corporation operated by a board of directors composed of members elected by and from the residents of that RCA. The 29 RCAs then collectively form the Homes Associations of Country Club District which has a ten member board of directors selected from among the authorized representatives of the member associations. The umbrella RCA is responsible for the maintenance work for each of the member RCAs and each RCA contributes its pro-rata share of the maintenance expenses (Urban Land Institute 1964). However, most RCAs are not this complex. They typically involve a single association operating independently of other associations (ACIR 1989).

RCAs are also sometimes distinguished as being either territorial or nonterritorial types. Over 90 percent of RCAs are the territorial type. They manage common real estate, such as open spaces, park land, parking lots, streets, and sidewalks, and have defined boundaries, like a municipality. Nonterritorial RCAs are those that include only high-rise buildings or sets of units on individual lots. These RCAs have little or no responsibility for open land and associated facilities and are rarely involved in the land-use regulation and service provision activities that characterize the territorial RCA (ACIR 1989). This book focuses on territorial RCAs because they are the most prevalent and they look and act more like local governments than nonterritorial RCAs. Because of their broader range of services, they are also more likely to interact with local governments.

Extent, Location, and Size of RCAs

Unfortunately, there is no reliable inventory to accurately determine the extent of RCAs in the United States. Even within most localities the actual number of RCAs is usually not known by local officials. The U.S. Census Bureau does keep national statistics for condominium developments but it does not identify separately the number of housing units or individuals subject to RCA governance. At the present time, the best source for determining the extent of RCAs in the United States is the membership list of the Community Associations Institute (CAI).

CAI was created in 1973 by the Urban Land Institute and the National Association of Homebuilders. It is intended to be a neutral source of information on how to successfully create, operate, and govern RCAs (Dowden 1989). However, CAI membership is voluntary and because there are membership dues many of the nation's smaller RCAs have decided not to join. As a result, CAI's membership list (approximately 13,000 RCAs) significantly understates the actual number of RCAs in the United States. Thus, the only numbers available concerning how many RCAs there are in the United States and how many people are governed by them are estimates made by CAI researchers.

According to CAI estimates, in 1960 there were fewer than 1,000 RCAs in the United States, with the majority of them located in California and Florida. In 1988 they estimated that the number of RCAs had increased to over 130,000 nationwide, covering more than 12 percent of the nation's households and 30 million people (Dowden 1989). They also noted that more than 50 percent of all housing for sale in the 50 largest metropolitan areas in the country and nearly all new residential development in California, Florida, New York, Texas, and suburban Washington, D.C., is governed by a RCA. Based on recent housing starts and the continued popularity of RCA-governed housing developments, the CAI also estimated that the total number of RCAs will reach approximately 225,000 by the year 2000 (Community Associations Institute 1988). Assuming that these new RCAs are approximately the same size as existing RCAs (230 residents per RCA), more than 50 million Americans will be subject to RCA governance in the year 2000.

According to a recent nationwide survey of CAI's membership, although RCAs are still concentrated on the east and west coasts, they are now found in all regions of the country. They tend to be especially prominent in suburban (62%) and urban areas (30%). They are less likely to be present in rural areas (8%) (see Table 2.1).

RCAs range in size from fewer than 10 residents located on a

Table 2.1
Characteristics of CAI-Member Residential Community Associations Responding to a Nationwide 1990 Survey

Type of Association	
Condominium	61%
Homeowners	35
Cooperative	1
Others	3
	100%
Location	
Suburban	62%
Urban	30
Rural	8
	100%
*Region**	
Northeast	17%
South	26
Midwest	13
West	44
	100%

*The membership list of the Community Associations Institute was used to generate this survey's sample. Their membership list may underestimate the number of residential community associations located in the Northeast.

Source: National survey of CAI-Member residential community associations conducted by the author.

single city street to as many as 68,000 in thousands of homes and condominiums covering hundreds of acres. A 1988 survey of CAI-member RCAs conducted by the U.S. Advisory Commission on Intergovernmental Relations revealed that the typical RCA consisted of 153 units. However, since CAI membership is skewed toward the larger associations who can afford the organization's dues, the actual size of the typical association is probably smaller than 153 units (ACIR 1989). A random survey of California RCAs conducted in 1986 revealed that RCAs there have an average size of 43 units (Barton and Silverman 1987a). Given the acknowledged bias of ACIR's sample, the 43–unit average discovered in California is probably more indicative of the typical size of RCAs nationwide.

RCAs' Four Basic Operational Functions

Regardless of their location or size, all RCAs share four basic operational functions. First, through a board of directors elected by the community's homeowners, they maintain commonly owned neighborhood amenities, such as swimming pools, tennis courts, and park and picnic areas. Second, they arrange for the delivery of the services specified in their articles of incorporation or for services subsequently approved by the homeowners according to the procedures described in their bylaws. Many of the services that are specified in RCAs' articles of incorporation are normally provided by local governments. They were included by the developer as part of the negotiation process with the local government's planning officials when the development was considered for approval. Although the number and type of these services vary from one RCA to another, as Table 2.2 indicates, most provide lawn care, trash collection, water and sewer services, street and sidewalk repair, parking lot maintenance, and, in colder climates, snow removal. In urban areas, many also supply private neighborhood security patrols. As Table 2.3 shows, the typical RCA provides its members with 12 services, with the number of services ranging from a low of 1 to a high of 19.

Although the number and type of services provided by RCAs helps to gauge the scope of their activities, these figures reveal

Table 2.2
Services Provided by CAI-Member Residential Community Associations Responding to a Nationwide 1990 Survey

Services Frequently Considered Governmental Functions	
Lawn care in common areas	92%
Tree/shrubbery care	91
Trash collection	74
Water or sewer	65
Street repair	53
Street lighting	51
Snow removal	50
Sidewalks	50
Recreational areas	36
Security patrol	34
Playground/tot lot	27
Lake or beach	13
Services Frequently Considered Private Functions	
Painting/outside maintenance	77%
Parking lot repair	76
Gates or fences	63
Swimming pool	62
Tennis courts	32
Indoor community center	29

Source: National survey of CAI-member residential community associations conducted by the author.

relatively little about the nature or quality of the relationship between community associations and their membership. To get a better sense of this relationship, a nationwide survey of RCA board of directors' members was conducted in 1990. The board members were asked to indicate how they thought their association's membership would rate the association's performance as a service provider. Thirty-two percent of the respondents believed that their membership would rate the association's performance in delivering services as excellent and 63 percent indicated that the membership would rate the association's performance as good. Only 4

Table 2.3
Number of Services Provided by CAI-Member Residential Community Associations Responding to a Nationwide 1990 Survey

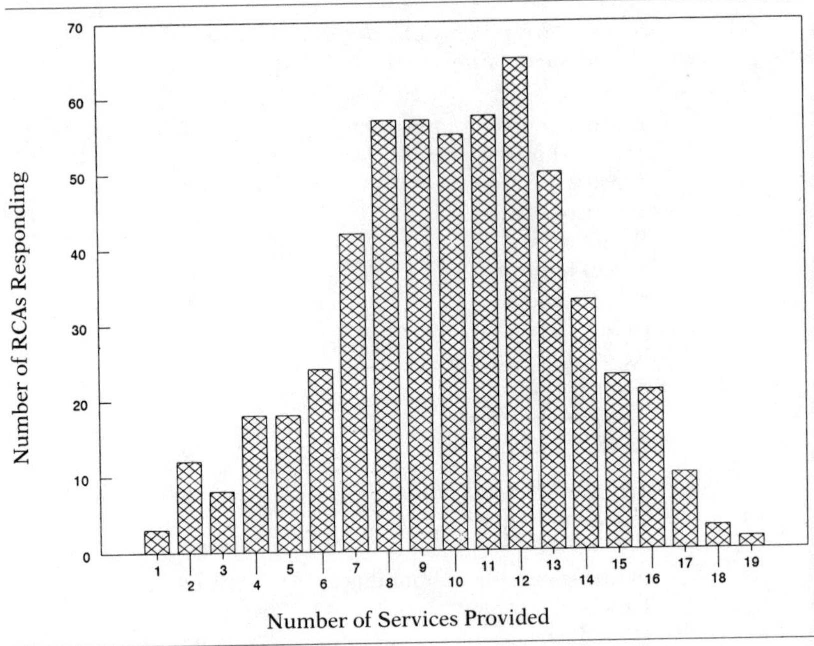

Source: National survey of CAI-Member residential community associations conducted by the author.

percent of the respondents indicated that their members would rate the association's performance as a service provider as fair and only 1 percent believed that their members would rate the association's performance as being poor (Dilger 1990).

It can be asserted that RCA board members are likely to overestimate their memberships' satisfaction with their association's performance as a service provider because they are, at least indirectly as board members, responsible for service delivery. However, the very high percentage of respondents indicating a belief that their membership would rate their community association as either a good or excellent service provider (95%) suggests that the typical RCA member is relatively satisfied with their RCA's performance as a service provider.

The 1990 survey also asked if there were any specific services currently offered by their community association that could be provided more efficiently by local government. An overwhelming majority of respondents (78%) said no. Of those who did believe that local government could provide one or more of their services more efficiently than their RCA, the most frequently named services were street lighting (78 respondents), street repair (77 respondents), and trash collection (31 respondents).

RCAs' third operational function is to tax its members through regular and special assessments to pay for the provision of the association's amenities and services. The developer sets the initial assessment fees until the RCA is turned over to the homeowners (usually when 75% of the homes are sold and, increasingly, when at least 50% of the homes are sold). The RCA's board of directors, subject to the procedures outlined in their bylaws, then determine the assessment fees. Typically, the bylaws give the board of directors the authority to increase the association's assessment fees each year by an amount equal to the national rate of inflation without securing the approval of the general membership. Any increases beyond the rate of inflation are usually subject to the approval of two-thirds or three-quarters of the homeowners present at a general meeting of the RCA's entire membership (Dowden 1986). Because RCAs are so diverse in terms of both size and level of services provided, they charge a wide range of assessment fees. The ACIR's 1988 survey of CAI-member RCAs discovered that RCA assessments ranged from under $100 annually to over $5,000 annually. The typical RCA assessment was $336 annually (ACIR 1989).

RCAs' fourth operational function is to protect the neighborhood's aesthetics and real estate values by enforcing the covenants, conditions, and restrictions (CC&Rs) that are attached to each home's deed. Like government's policing powers, which impose restrictions on private rights to enhance the public welfare, order, and security, the CC&Rs empower the association's board of directors to impose restrictions on private rights to enhance the neighborhood's welfare. The CC&Rs often empower the board of directors to decide what color homeowners can paint their house or condominium, what kind and how many vehicles they can park in front of their yard, whether they can build an addition onto their home, how often they must mow their lawn, and whether they can have a television antenna on the roof of their home (ACIR 1988).

Several studies have indicated that property values of neighborhoods governed by RCAs fare better in the long run than those of virtually identical neighborhoods lacking covenants to prevent physical deterioration (Frazier 1984, 1989). However, some of RCAs' critics have questioned RCAs' ability to enhance property values in urban areas. They argue that it is generally assumed that RCAs enhance property values in urban areas by shielding low-density residential uses from the encroachment of industrial, commercial, and, in some instances, from multi-family residential uses. However, given the large number of factors affecting property values in urban areas, it is difficult to prove that segregating land uses necessarily enhances residential property values. Moreover, these critics suggest that segregating low-density residential land uses from commercial land uses and multi-family residential uses can effectively segregate social and economic classes, isolating RCA residents from those who neither live, shop, nor work with them. As a result, they fear that RCAs' segregation of land uses will result in heightened feelings of mutual hostility and suspicion among different economic classes, races, and ethnic groups because land use segregation decreases access to other kinds of people and activities, causing many to perceive outsiders as being undesirable. Instead of segregating land uses, these critics advocate the thoughtful integration of various types of residential development with nonresidential land uses. In this way, people from different economic, social, and racial backgrounds will be encouraged to interact and learn from one another (Winokur 1989b).

Although there is no consensus on the impact that RCAs have on social tolerance, most analysts do agree that, in most instances, the enforcement of RCAs' CC&Rs do enhance property values in RCA-governed neighborhoods. However, they also agree that the enforcement of the CC&Rs is the single greatest source of tension and conflict within RCAs. Most homeowners recognize their RCA's authority to enforce the CC&Rs and support the restrictions as they apply to others but complain bitterly if they are cited for a violation. Many have even resorted to litigation to preserve what they view as their right to do whatever they want with their property (Barton and Silverman 1989; Winokur 1989b).

The Fifth Function: Lobbying

The typical RCA's articles of incorporation, bylaws, and declaration of covenants will not mention lobbying as one of its functions. However, because local governments directly affect the welfare of RCA members through their taxing, zoning, and service delivery functions, it would seem reasonable to assume that RCAs regularly attempt to influence the outcome of local government decisions. Recognizing this, the U.S. Advisory Commission on Intergovernmental Relations (ACIR) included several questions in its 1988 nationwide survey of RCA board members that were designed to determine the extent of RCA-local government interactions. Debra Dean summarized the results of ACIR's survey in her article "Community Associations and Local Government Relationships: Attitudes and Services," which appeared in the May/June 1989 issue of *Common Ground*. She reported that:

1. There was considerable overlap between the services provided by community associations and local governments.
2. Community associations and local governments have contact about relatively few services and, to the extent that contacts do exist, they appear to be initiated by the community association.
3. Although community association officials generally believe that local governments treat them fairly, one out of every ten community associations described the cooperation between themselves and local government as "poor."

Dean also wrote that ACIR's survey suggested that RCAs generally do not attempt to influence local governments on a regular basis:

> For 11 of . . . 13 services, a majority of associations reported that they had not attempted to influence local government. This suggests that the typical relationship between a community association and local government is, as one respondent put it, "We leave them alone and they leave us alone" (Dean 1989).

She also indicated that when RCAs did attempt to influence local governments the most frequently cited issues discussed were police protection and the location of stop lights and stop signs.

Using ACIR's survey as a starting point, and with the assistance of the Community Associations Institute, this author mailed a second nationwide survey to CAI-member RCAs in 1990. It was designed to further our understanding of RCAs' role in providing services that are traditionally offered by local governments and to determine the extent and nature of their efforts to influence local government decisions.

The 1990 survey was mailed to 1,100 RCA board members who are also members of the CAI. Five hundred and sixty-one surveys were returned for a response rate of 51 percent. Like ACIR's survey, this one focused on territorial RCAs because they are the most prevalent and have characteristics and functions similar to local governments. Specifically, both the ACIR survey and the 1990 survey refer to RCAs with the following three characteristics:

1. The organization is territorial in scope. That is, it encompasses a plot of land, including buildings, open spaces, and parking lots, and has defined boundaries, much like a municipality.
2. The covenants creating the community association include mandatory membership and mandatory fees for home or lot owners, as well as rules governing resident behavior, particularly with regard to the exterior characteristics of residences.
3. The organization is responsible for the regulation and management of common areas and the provision of services such as maintenance of recreational areas and facilities, parking lots, streets, and sidewalks.

The 1990 survey results suggest that while RCAs' lobbying efforts are not viewed by RCA board members as being one of their RCA's primary functions, RCAs are more active in the political arena than ACIR's survey results suggested. Seventy percent of the RCA board members who responded to the 1990 survey indicated that they regularly monitored local government actions and 63 percent replied that they had personally attended at least one local government meeting on behalf of their RCA during the preceding year. Moreover, 78 percent of the respondents indicated that someone from their association had either called or written to a local government official on behalf of the association in the past year. The number of issues discussed ranged from 1 to 10, with the most frequently cited number of issues discussed during the preceding year (1989) being 2. Traffic led the list of issues discussed (161 respondents) followed by zoning concerns, police protection, development issues, water and sewer services, and trash collection (see Table 2.4 for details).

The 1990 survey results suggest that while many RCA board members may prefer to a have a "we leave them alone and they leave us alone" relationship with their local government, most of them recognize the potential influence of local government decisions on their association and have an ongoing, if somewhat wary, relationship with their local government. When asked to evaluate this relationship, 16 percent of the respondents indicated that their association's relationship with their local government was excellent, 46 percent indicated that it was good, 15 percent said fair, 4 percent said poor, and 19 percent indicated that they had no relationship with their local government (Dilger 1990).

Table 2.4
Issues Discussed By CAI-Member Residential Community Associations With Local Government Officials in 1989*

Traffic	29%
Zoning	27
Police protection	26
Development issues	22
Water or sewer services	19
Trash collection	17
Taxes	16
Animal control	15
Parking	14
Parks	10
Schools	6

*Cumulative percentages exceed 100 because some respondents discussed more than one issue with local government officials.

Source: National survey of CAI-member residential community associations conducted by the author.

Intergovernmental Activities and Issues

Because they are private organizations, RCAs will never be regarded as full partners in the intergovernmental system of governance. However, their increasing numbers and interactions with local governments make them important actors in that system. Moreover, although public finance statistics compiled by the national government do not include estimates of how much money RCAs are spending on "public" services, their increasing numbers and the results of recent surveys concerning the scope of their service activities suggest that RCAs account for the most significant privatization of local government responsibilities in recent times (ACIR 1989). As a result, state and local policymakers are increasingly aware that RCA activities raise many issues that impact the intergovernmental system of governance. Typically, these issues fall within one of five general categories: taxation, finances, service provision, citizenship and governance, and consumer protection.

Taxation. RCAs pose a number of taxation issues for both their members and for local governments. One of the most contentious of these issues involves tax equity. RCA members are assessed a special fee for the services they receive from their RCA. At the same time, they also pay local property taxes at the same rate as other property owners in their town or city. Although a portion of their assessment fees is used for services that directly benefit only the members of the association and are not normally provided by government, such as exterior maintenance of buildings and exclusive use of a swimming pool or clubhouse, a portion of the assessment fees are used to pay for services that local government provides to other members of the community without any additional charge beyond their property tax collections. Thus, RCA members are often taxed by local government for services, such as snow or trash removal, that they have already paid for and provided themselves. RCA members not only view this as being unfair, but argue that it defeats one of the prime reasons for creating RCAs in the first place, to provide affordable housing. To promote tax equity and the financial attractiveness of purchasing a home in a PUD or condominium development, they want local governments to follow the example set by Houston, Texas, Kansas City, Missouri, and Montgomery County, Maryland, which grant RCA members a property tax rebate commensurate with the cost savings realized from the RCA's provision of services.

Given their difficult financial positions, most local governments have refused a tax rebate for RCA members. Because increased intergovernmental funding from either the national or their state governments is not a viable option for most local governments, providing a tax rebate for RCA members would require them to either raise local taxes or reduce services in other areas of their town or city. Neither of these options is politically attractive. However, as the number of RCA members nationwide continue to increase, tax rebates are certain to become an important political issue in many local campaigns.

Another tax equity issue arises for members of homeowners' associations (HOAs). In HOAs, the association owns common property and is responsible for paying property taxes on it. These payments are funded through association assessment fees. Individual homeowners also pay property taxes on their residences. In many communities, the local tax assessor will reflect the added value of common facilities onto the value of the individual's home. As a result, depending on local assessment practices, HOA members may be assessed twice for living in a RCA, once when paying their share of the common property's property tax bill and a second time through a higher appraised value on their home (ACIR 1989). To promote tax equity, HOA members want local assessment practices to stop what is, in their view, double taxation.

Another tax equity issue involves the national government. It allows taxpayers to deduct their property taxes from their taxable income when determining their national tax liability. RCA members are not allowed to deduct their association fees from their taxable income even though a portion of their fees are used to provide services similar to those provided by property tax dollars. To promote tax equity, RCA members want the national government to allow them to deduct from their taxable income the portion of their assessment fees used to pay for services that are provided by their local government to other residents in their community (ACIR 1988; Frazier 1984).

Finances. Another issue involving RCAs and intergovernmental policymakers is what responsibility, if any, local governments have in the event a RCA in their jurisdiction goes bankrupt or is otherwise unable to provide services to its members. Although relatively few RCAs have ever gone bankrupt, many have approached local governments asking for fiscal assistance following an unforeseen financial setback, such as a water-main break (Dowden 1980; Longhini and Mosena 1978). During the 1970s and, to a lesser extent during the early 1980s, some RCAs ran into financial difficulty because some developers set initial assessment fees artificially low to entice buyers to purchase homes in the subdivision. Once the RCA was turned over to the homeowners they realized that the fees were too low to maintain adequate reserves. These RCAs ran into financial difficulty when they were unable to get their membership to agree to raise the assessment fees to realistic levels. This resistance came about primarily because the membership was predominantly "house poor," having little disposable income left after purchasing their new homes.

Although local governments are not required by any legal statute to provide services to a neighborhood whose association runs into financial difficulty, most local governments have enacted specific ordinances dealing with RCAs that allow them to step in and provide services if a financial difficulty or emergency should arise. In the absence of a specific ordinance dealing with RCAs, many local governments have generic ordinances that allow them to perform maintenance functions on private property if the public health, safety, or welfare is threatened. In both instances, local governments generally do not use public funds to provide these services. Instead, they assess the individual unit owners the cost of providing the services (Dowden 1980).

Ironically, although local governments provide mechanisms to take over common areas and infrastructure costs from financially troubled RCAs, most do not regulate RCA finances in any way (Dowden 1980). Many do not even require developers to post performance bonds to ensure that they will finish promised facilities, such as swimming pools, tennis courts, and club houses (ACIR 1989). Because local governments are potentially affected by RCA financial activities, some have argued that they should require developers to post performance bonds prior to construction to ensure that they will construct promised facilities. They have also argued that all RCAs should be required to periodically report their financial status to local officials and to meet certain financial tests, such as required reserves.

Service Provision. Because a RCA contracts privately for services, it decides how much service it wants and how much it is willing to pay for it. This often results in differences in service levels between RCA and non-RCA residential subdivisions within a single public jurisdiction. For example, it is not uncommon for local governments to set priorities for snow removal on the basis of street usage. Heavily used highways are typically cleared first, residential streets last. Because RCAs contract privately for snow removal, their residential streets are often cleared of snow before other residential streets in the area. In addition, RCAs may offer services, such as ride sharing or the provision of certain recreational facilities, that may not be available to other residents in the area. Where there is sufficient variety in service levels among RCAs and between RCAs and non-RCA subdivisions within local jurisdictions, the home buyers' decision on where to purchase their home will be affected (ACIR 1989). This "voting with their feet" phenomena has many important implications for local government policymakers. It can alter the local government's fiscal condition as home buyers choose to locate in one jurisdiction over another as they search for what they view as the optimal service provision/cost situation. It can alter the geographical distribution of wealth within a community as home buyers (generally the more fiscally secure portion of the population) alter their locational decisions based on RCA ownership. This, in turn, can alter the locational decisions of businesses, affecting employment patterns as well as local sales and property tax revenue. In addition, the existence of RCAs can alter the community's climate of expectations concerning service levels, where citizens come to expect different levels of "free" governmental services depending upon what services their neighbors receive in an RCA-governed neighborhood.

Another service-related issue involves citizen access to local government services. Local governments often refuse to provide RCA neighborhoods with services that they routinely supply to other neighborhoods within their jurisdiction. They refuse because they are reluctant to have their employees venture onto private property in the fear that they may incur liability in case of an accident. For example, local government animal control officers generally will not enter onto RCA property without prior, written permission. Similarly, unless specific prior, written agreements have been entered into, local police will not patrol RCA streets or enforce parking or traffic regulations on them. Moreover, local governments often refuse to collect trash from RCA neighborhoods. In addition to the liability issue, many smaller towns refuse to collect RCA neighborhood trash because they often lack the special equipment necessary to empty large dumpsters (ACIR 1989).

The existence of private streets and parking facilities also affects the behavior of local government officials because they impact traffic and parking patterns in the surrounding community. For example, if a street that is owned and maintained by a RCA is used by commuters as a shortcut, the RCA could decide to install speed bumps on the street or close it to the public in an effort to protect the interests of its members. RCAs can, and typically do, make these decisions without conferring with or even informing local government officials. These decisions, of course, affect local traffic flows and, in turn, local government's decisions concerning street widths, location of stop signs, and traffic signals (ACIR 1989).

Another issue involving RCA service provision relates to development standards. Local governments typically specify design and construction standards for public facilities. At one time, developers built streets and parks to public specifications and then dedicated them to the local government. Increasingly, developers are meeting public standards for construction but not design, and keeping the facilities under private ownership through RCAs. If an RCA should experience financial difficulty in the future, the noncompliance with public design standards could create a problem if the facility had to be dedicated to the local government. There has been little evidence of RCA financial failures, but the issue does exist as a concern for local government officials (ACIR 1989).

Citizenship and Governance. Many RCAs, particularly ones with more than 100 units, are incorporated and, obviously, are bound by the provisions of corporate law that exist in the jurisdiction where they are located. Although corporate law varies to a certain extent from state to state, three principles generally apply in all states. First, in order for the actions of RCA board members and their representatives to be valid (many larger RCAs hire a professional manager or management company to implement the board's policies), they must not exceed the scope of their authority as indicated in state law and in the RCA's bylaws. Second, RCA board members and their representatives must adhere to the business judgment rule which states that they must act in good faith, in a manner that is in the best interests of the corporation, and must act with such care as an ordinarily prudent person in a like position should use under similar circumstances. Finally, board members and their representatives have a fiduciary duty to the corporation (Rosenberry 1985, 1989). This forbids board members and their representatives from using their authority to enhance their own position at the expense of the association, requires them to disclose everything that may be relevant to their relationship to the association, creates an obligation of confidentiality on behalf of the association toward all third parties, and mandates a responsibility to show reasonable care, diligence, and skill when acting on behalf of the association (Diaz 1988).

State courts have generally held unincorporated RCAs to these same legal standards. They do this because, regardless of the RCA's size or whether the developer that created it actually filed articles of incorporation, all RCAs have business responsibilities that involve numerous duties including the upkeep of common property, the preparation and maintenance of budgets and records, and the assessment of owners' shares of common expenses.

Although the courts have had little difficulty in applying corporate law to RCAs, they have had a very hard time determining whether constitutional controls over state actions apply to RCAs and their board of directors. The legal distinction between state action and private action has important consequences for determining the legal standards applied to RCA's governing structures.

Recognizing that RCAs have both business and governmental characteristics, state courts have generally ruled that RCAs' internal governance structures are not subject to the strict legal standards applied to government officials. However, they also have ruled that RCAs' operating rules and procedures must meet a higher legal standard than the one applied to businesses. RCAs' standard, referred to as the legal "rule of reasonableness," allows RCAs' internal rules and procedures to violate many constitutional edicts applied to government officials (Hyatt and Downer 1987; Hyatt 1988). For example, although RCAs may appear to represent the essence of local democracy and participation, voting within most RCAs is based on home ownership rather than residence. As a result, although renters in RCA-governed neighborhoods are directly affected by the RCA's decisions, they are often not allowed to participate in the RCA's decisionmaking processes. Renters are often purposively disenfranchised in the neighborhood's CC&Rs because they have an incentive to oppose efforts to increase the neighborhood's property values. Increased property values could result in rent increases (ACIR 1988). Instead of allowing renters to participate in RCA governance, absentee owners are made voting members of the association and investors who own more than one unit have more than one vote. Moreover, most HOAs give one vote to each lot owner rather than to each adult resident and most COAs give a weighted vote to the owners of each condominium unit based on either the unit's value or its square footage. All these voting mechanisms violate the principle of one person, one vote articulated in *Reynolds v. Sims* (1964), *Avery v. Midland County* (1968) and *Hadley v. Junior College District* (1970) that applies to governmental entities.

The practice of basing suffrage on home ownership instead of residence affects the internal political dynamics of RCAs in a way that diminishes their capacity to act as facilitators of civic virtue. Disenfranchised renters have little incentive to participate in RCA governance and absentee owners are typically less interested in the RCAs' day-to-day operations than resident owners, are less likely to actively engage in its governance structure, and are less likely to vote on association matters (Barton and Silverman 1988). Under such circumstances, it is not surprising that relatively few residents become actively involved in RCA governance (see Chapter 7 for an extended discussion of RCA governance issues).

Consumer Protection. Although little systematic evidence exists, there is strong anecdotal evidence to suggest that many home buyers in RCA- governed neighborhoods do not understand the extent of their obligations prior to purchasing their homes. For example, an appraiser for the U.S. Department of Housing and Urban Development estimated that as many as 85 percent of homeowners in RCA-governed communities are not aware of the full extent of their neighborhood's CC&Rs (Winokur 1989b). This ignorance is largely attributed to the lack of state action. Only half the states require developers to disclose the RCA's CC&Rs to new home buyers and even fewer require disclosure of the CC&Rs on resale (ACIR 1989). Moreover, even when the CC&Rs are disclosed, they are often written in complex, legal language and are very long. As a result, even when disclosed, many home buyers do not read or fully understand the neighborhood's CC&Rs prior to purchasing their homes. Faced with a pile of papers to sign at closing, many people blindly sign whatever is put before them, not realizing that they are subject to the neighborhood's CC&Rs or the directives of an RCA. They become aware of the extent of the CC&Rs and the powers of the RCA's board of directors only when that board cites them as being in violation of the CC&Rs. Surprised homeowners often react negatively to the board's orders to comply with the CC&Rs. Heated words have often been exchanged and occasionally punches have been thrown. There have even been instances when the police were required to restore order (Miller 1990). Often, these disputes end up in the local consumer protection office or in the courts (Barton and Silverman 1989; Winokur 1989b). In an effort to promote consumer awareness, some have suggested that local governments should require developers to fully disclose the neighborhood's CC&Rs to prospective new home buyers prior to closing and to require all subsequent owners to fully disclose the neighborhood's CC&Rs when they sell their home to others (ACIR 1989; Winokur 1989b).

Another consumer protection issue concerns disclosure of the RCA's financial condition. Many RCAs are responsible for the maintenance of common facilities that may require large capital expenses to renovate or repair. Examples of such facilities are streets, sewer lines, club houses, swimming pools, and roofs of multi-unit buildings. Maintenance of these facilities is often funded out of the RCA's reserves. If these reserves are inadequate, a large special assessment may become necessary to make needed repairs. This is particularly true of RCAs formed during the 1950s and 1960s. As their infrastructure ages, their members face major renovation tasks (Peterson 1990). Potential buyers of homes in RCA-governed communities often are not aware of the financial condition of the association, or of the condition of the association's facilities. Some have suggested that states and local governments should follow the example set by California, New York, and Virginia which require sellers of homes in RCA-governed neighborhoods to provide all potential purchasers with a public offering statement. This statement usually includes a copy of the RCA's bylaws and CC&Rs as well as a summary of the RCA's financial condition and current assessment fees. The buyers are then given a cooling-off period to allow them an opportunity to review the material and rescind their purchase agreements. California also requires its RCAs to conduct a reserve study that estimates the useful life of relevant common facilities and to include the study in the public offering statement (Isaacson and Segal 1981; ACIR 1989).

Arguments for RCAs

Some scholars applaud the emergence of RCAs as an opportunity for people of similar backgrounds and values to join together to create a strong sense of community at the local level. They are convinced that the public's dissatisfaction or alienation toward governmental performance is at least partly attributable to a loss of community spirit. Government, they contend, is often remote and bureaucratic and, as a result, inefficient and wasteful. RCAs, in contrast, provide an opportunity for direct democracy where neighbors meet face to face to resolve problems. This interaction, it is argued, promotes a stronger sense of civic virtue because neighbors recognize the efficacy of their participation in RCA meetings. As the Urban Land Institute put it in one of their studies,

> The explosive growth of our cities, their trend to giantism, and the high mobility of their residents are rapidly destroying a sense of community among individuals in urban America. . . . The best possible way to bring about—or to revive—a grass roots sense of community is for home owners to control nearby facilities of importance to them and through this to participate actively in the life of their neighborhoods (Urban Land Institute 1964).

RCAs' advocates also argue that RCAs should be encouraged because they provide substantial economic benefits to both consumers and local governments. They benefit consumers by offering them greater choice in determining the level of neighborhood services and amenities that they pay for. In addition, RCAs supply these services and amenities in a more cost effective way than government because they routinely contract out their services on a competitive basis to private service providers. They also enhance property values by enforcing the neighborhood's CC&Rs and preventing physical deterioration. In several urban areas, RCAs' ability to close neighborhood streets to public traffic has proven effective in combating crime and raising property values (Nelson 1989; Frazier 1989).

RCAs benefit government by freeing it of its financial responsibilities for maintaining streets, sewers, and other infrastructure, for providing services such as trash collection and snow removal, and for providing and maintaining amenities such as open spaces and recreational facilities. RCAs' enhancement of property values also serves to augment local government's property tax revenue.

Arguments Opposing RCAs

Other scholars view RCAs more critically. They fail to see how RCAs will promote a sense of community spirit or enhance civic virtue when many deny voting privileges to renters and have governance procedures that violate the constitutional standards applied to government. They want government to regulate RCAs to ensure that they are run in a democratic fashion and are in full accord with the constitutional guarantees embodied in the First and Fourteenth Amendments.

RCAs' critics also question the assumption that RCAs provide consumers greater choice in determining the level of neighborhood services and amenities that they pay for. Although RCAs do provide more consumer options in the abstract, in many areas of the country RCAs now dominate the local housing market and are increasingly offering fairly uniform levels and types of services. As a result, the service options available to consumers have narrowed in recent years (Barton and Silverman 1989; Winokur 1989b). Moreover, RCAs' critics question the assertion that homeowners are freely and knowingly consenting to restrictions on their property rights in exchange for enhanced property values. As mentioned previously, many consumers are not fully aware of the RCAs' powers or their own role in RCA governance when they purchase their home. As a result, the homeowners' consent to the RCAs' CC&Rs is often reduced to a purely theoretical premise and, unfortunately, often does not reflect their autonomous will (Winokur 1989b). To promote consumer protection and enhance the legitimacy of RCA governance, RCAs' critics want all states to require sellers of homes subject to RCA governance to provide potential buyers with comprehensive public offering statements prior to closing and to give them a cooling-off period to allow purchasers an opportunity to read the statement and rescind their purchase agreements. The statements should include a copy of the RCA's articles of incorporation, bylaws, and declaration of covenants, and an accounting of the RCA's fiscal condition. They also want states to require sales personnel to be more forthcoming about the precise nature of the RCA's governance procedures and CC&Rs in the early stages of the sales process (Barton and Silverman 1989).

Some of RCAs' critics also question the assumption that RCAs necessarily enhance property values and, by inference, promote an aesthetically pleasing landscape. They note that RCAs enhance property values primarily by preventing neighbors from using their property in odd or eccentric ways and by protecting the neighborhood from the encroachment of commercial, industrial, or higher density residential uses. However, the empirical evidence concerning the impact of segregating land uses in urban areas on property values is inconclusive (Winokur 1989b). In addition, although they admit that the enforcement of neighborhood CC&Rs can produce residential areas of striking beauty, they also argue that RCAs have contributed to much of the suburban sprawl in the United States that is aesthetically undifferentiated and culturally desolate. Moreover, as mentioned previously, some of these critics maintain that by segregating land uses, RCAs effectively segregate social and economic classes and may serve to hinder social, economic, and racial tolerance.

RCAs' critics also dispute the notion that RCAs are necessarily better service providers than government. They note that many RCAs, particularly smaller ones, lack the resources and scale necessary to bargain effectively with contractors. Moreover, they are convinced that local governments should not abdicate their financial responsibilities for infrastructure maintenance and delivery of services to RCAs because RCAs operate according to the principal of fiscal equivalence, where individual homeowners pay for the services and amenities they receive regardless of their ability to pay. This principal prohibits RCAs from redistributing costs among its members. If a member suffers an economic loss and can no longer afford to pay the assessment fee, even if the member voted against the provision of services or amenities, RCAs are required to collect the fee and, as a last resort, can place a lien against the member's home. RCAs' critics argue that state and local governments should retain their financial responsibilities because they can protect those who suffer an economic loss by redistributing government expenses among income groups. Local governments are able to redistribute expenses by providing those with modest incomes property tax relief through the use of property tax "circuit breakers." Thirty-six states currently offer a circuit-breaker program. They typically involve a rebate of the property taxes paid or a credit against the individual's state income tax obligation (ACIR 1991). RCA's critics argue that state and local governments can then impose progressive income tax structures to recapture these "lost" revenues from others in the community.

Finally, RCAs' critics argue that when local governments abdicate their responsibility for providing services and other public amenities to RCAs, they also abdicate their role in creating affordable housing. Instead of emphasizing the formation of RCAs that often have assessment fees prohibitively expensive for those with modest incomes, they believe that local governments should use their zoning authority to allow developers to build houses on smaller lot sizes, to reduce development costs and housing prices, and then place public parks and other recreational amenities within walking distance of these homes. In this way, people of modest means can buy a home and have access to desirable amenities without the burden of assessment fees. As one report put it,

> We suggest that [RCAs are] a troubled and overused form of government. As entry-level housing in many areas becomes increasingly restricted to [RCAs], government needs to encourage alternatives, such as creative use of small lots and use of public roads and parks to make entry-level housing without common property possible in areas of high land costs (Barton and Silverman 1989).

The remaining chapters in this book will explore these pro and con arguments in depth, examine the factors that led to the recent proliferation of RCAs, determine their role in providing public services, consider their implications for local politics, and speculate about their ramifications for American governance.

3

RCAs' Historical Development

Residential community associations have a long history as an acknowledged form of property ownership in Europe. Homeowners' associations (HOAs) have existed there for over two hundred and fifty years. The first HOA was created after the Earl of Leicester built a townhouse in London in the early 1600s and constructed a park in front of it. By 1700 the park was surrounded by buildings and the neighborhood had became known as Leicester Square. In 1743 the property owners in Leicester Square created the first homeowners' association to assure themselves the exclusive use and perpetual maintenance of the park (Urban Land Institute 1964).

Condominium associations have an even longer history than homeowners' associations in Europe. Archaeologists have determined that condominiums were prevalent in major Roman cities as early as the sixth century B.C. (Dowden 1980). However, condominium associations have a somewhat shorter history in the United States. They did not gain widespread acceptance among American home buyers until the 1960s. As a result, the early history of residential community associations in the United States is primarily the history of homeowners' associations, with the first one appearing in 1844.

The 1800s: Homeowners' Associations Origins in the United States

With a few notable exceptions, the modern homeowners' association did not exist in the United States during the 1800s. At that time, land in settled areas was usually marked off into building lots and sold for whatever purposes the new owners intended. Home buyers were never quite certain what was going to be built on the parcel of land down the road or even on the land adjacent to their own. Although many home buyers may not have been very happy about the situation, the "buy at your own risk" principle prevailed. Subdividing large tracts of land exclusively for residential or commercial purposes presupposes a level of planning and control that was not the norm at that time. There were no public planning agencies or zoning codes as we know them today. The general pattern in rapidly urbanizing areas was for low-density residential neighborhoods to be converted slowly over time into higher density residential neighborhoods or commercial-industrial areas. Typically, this conversion process took approximately two decades to complete. Most property owners anticipated such changes and moved relatively frequently to keep one step ahead of the changing character of the neighborhood (Weiss and Watts 1989).

The relatively haphazard development patterns that took place during the 1800s slowly began to change as urban land developers moved away from just subdividing raw land into marketable plots and toward the more complex practices of residential subdivision development. Initially, this involved the installation of improvements, such as roads, and, in some cases, the construction of houses prior to the sale of the land. Some developers who built residential subdivisions for the more affluent home buyer also experimented with the provision of extensive landscaping and amenities, as well as with deed restrictions concerning the development and uses of property in the subdivision. It was hoped that these added amenities and restrictions would enhance sales among those home buyers seeking a more exclusive lifestyle. Although these deed restrictions would serve as forerunners for the modern community association's CC&Rs, they were enacted with the realization that it was inevitable that even the best neighborhood would eventually "decline" into higher density uses. For example, most of these restrictions were valid for only five to fifteen years, long enough to promise potential home buyers that the restrictions would protect the neighborhood's aesthetics while they lived in their homes but not long enough to warrant the establishment of a permanent homeowners' association to enforce them.

The restrictions' impact on the neighborhood's aesthetics was also limited because the main enforcement mechanism at that time was for neighboring property owners subject to the same restrictions to sue violators in civil court. Using the courts to enforce the deed restrictions was not very effective. First, this left enforcement to chance. If none of the neighboring property owners had the time, money, or initiative to sue, then the violation would proceed unchallenged. Second, by the time the civil suit got to court the violations usually had already done their damage to the neighborhood's aesthetics. Reversing the violations, such as ordering the removal of a building prohibited by the deed restrictions, was difficult and costly. Courts at that time were hesitant to intervene in such situations and were as likely to declare the restrictions void as they were to enforce them (Weiss and Watts 1989).

There were a few notable exceptions to the relatively unstructured nature of residential development during the 1800s. In several urban areas, residential developers of fashionable homes began to emulate the London practice of subdividing relatively large parcels of land into residential plots and placing a park at the center of the development. The developer usually deeded the park to the city, making it responsible for the park's improvement and maintenance. In 1831, Samuel Ruggles created the precedent for the establishment of homeowners' associations in the United States when he built Gramercy Park, an exclusive residential development in New York City. Through a legal device still in effect, instead of vesting the title to the development's park to the city, he vested the title to trustees. The trustees were charged with the responsibility for maintaining the park for the benefit of the owners of the 66 plots of land that surrounded the park. Although these trustees did not constitute a homeowners' association per se, the idea of deeding property to an entity other than the city and for charging that entity with the responsibility for maintaining property for the exclusive use and benefit of surrounding homeowners was a new development that set the precedent for the establishment of HOAs in the United States.

The first homeowners' association in the United States was

established on July 8, 1844. At that time, the owners of the twenty-eight homesites abutting a park located at the center of Louisburg Square in Boston agreed to sign a recorded land agreement that established the Committee of the Proprietors of Louisburg Square. The Committee consisted of three persons, chosen from among the twenty-eight homeowners by majority vote. It was charged with the responsibility for improving and maintaining the park. The recorded land agreement was attached as part of the twenty-eight properties' deeds, remaining with the land in perpetuity. The agreement provided for an initial assessment of up to $150 per lot for immediate improvements to the park and for the imposition of additional assessments to pay a proportionate share of future maintenance expenses. The Committee continues to function today (Urban Land Institute 1964).

For the remainder of the nineteenth century only a few other homeowners' associations were created and the ones that were established were usually based on the Louisburg Square model, where their primary purpose was to preserve and enhance a small neighborhood park in a relatively small, exclusive, and fashionable residential neighborhood. Then, in 1891, The Roland Park Company in Baltimore began the first of a series of four large-scale residential subdivisions that would mark a new era in the history of homeowners' associations. The planning of each of these subdivisions benefited by the trials of its predecessors and, as a group, proved that there was a market for homes in neighborhoods with permanent covenants that placed restrictions on land uses and made homeowners responsible for enforcing those restrictions and maintaining commonly owned amenities such as streets, sewers, and parks (Urban Land Institute 1964).

Roland Park's 466 acres was subdivided in 1891 and included 1,230 homesites. Unlike other contemporary subdivisions, its streets, sewers, water supply system, and an interior park were owned and maintained by the homeowners in common and it had restrictive covenants that controlled what homeowners could do with their land. Developed by Edward H. Bouton and planned by the foremost landscape architect of the time, Frederick Law Olmsted, Roland Park dominated the market for gracious homes in the Baltimore region for nearly 60 years. It was the first of four contiguous residential developments built by The Roland Park Company with the relatively exclusive Guilford neighborhood (336 acres, 723 homesites) being subdivided in 1913, joined by Homeland (363 acres, 990 homesites) in 1924, and the more affordable Northwood subdivision (554 acres, 3,808 homesites) in 1932.

The covenants for Roland Park were initially written to last in perpetuity but after facing resistance from potential home buyers not accustomed to being told what they could or could not do with their property, The Roland Park Company subsequently established a twenty-year termination date for the covenants and did not develop a provision for their renewal. However, as home sales progressed and the homeowners in Roland Park became more accustomed to having protective covenants, many expressed a regret that the covenants were not permanent. Since the homeowners were becoming more receptive to having protective covenants in place, The Roland Park Company decided when it started its Guilford subdivision that the residents there would be provided an opportunity to renew their covenants at twenty-year intervals by a two-thirds vote. Later, as the covenants in both Roland Park and Guilford became recognized by potential home buyers in the Baltimore area as effective devices for maintaining property values, The Roland Park Company decided that it would be easier to sell homes in its Homeland and Northwood subdivisions if it could promise potential home buyers that the covenants were more permanent. As a result, the covenants in Homeland and Northwood were to be automatically renewed at twenty-year intervals unless canceled by a written agreement signed by the owners of at least half of the land area in the development (Urban Land Institute 1964).

Although The Roland Park Company established the marketability of protective covenants for relatively large residential subdivisions, when it subdivided Roland Park and Guilford it did not plan to turn over the enforcement of the neighborhood's covenants, the collection of the neighborhood's assessments, or the responsibility for maintaining the neighborhood's streets, sewers, or its parks to the homeowners. Instead, it reserved the right to assign the administration of the covenants and the collection of the assessments to an undesignated successor or assignee once a substantial percentage of the homes in the development had been sold. Consequently, the developer failed to establish a framework to either allow or encourage the residents to take over these functions when the development was substantially completed. As it turned out, The Roland Park Company continued to enforce Roland Park's covenants, collect its assessment fees, and maintain its infrastructure for eighteen years and in Guilford for twenty-six years before turning these functions over to the homeowners. This reflected, in large part, the homeowners' general satisfaction with the performance of the company in maintaining the neighborhood's aesthetics over the years. As a result, the first homeowners' association in Baltimore, The Roland Park Roads and Maintenance Corporation, was not formed until 1909 and the Guilford Association was not formed until 1939. However, the ability of The Roland Park Roads and Maintenance Corporation to effectively manage its covenant enforcement and infrastructure maintenance responsibilities convinced The Roland Park Company that it would be appropriate to allow the homeowners in its Homeland subdivision to start their homeowners' association just one year after the development was subdivided (1924), establishing the precedent for developers to turn over the association's responsibilities to the homeowners in a relatively short time (Urban Land Institute 1964).

Although Baltimore's first homeowners' association, The Roland Park Roads and Maintenance Corporation, was created almost as an afterthought, as a group the four Baltimore subdivisions and their respective homeowners' associations proved that the property values of residential subdivisions could be preserved by sound land planning, protective covenants with maintenance agreements, continuous guidance by the developing company and, later, by the neighborhood's residents (Urban Land Institute 1964). Other developers interested in using homeowners' associations as marketing tools viewed these four residential subdivisions as models to be emulated throughout the United States. They learned that many difficulties could be avoided by activating the homeowners' association prior to the sale of the first lot, keeping it under developer control in the early development stages to set sound operating patterns, and transferring control to the homeowners by the time construction was substantially completed. The Baltimore communities also set the precedent for blanket restrictions that ran with the land so that new purchasers of homes in the subdivision could not opt out of the system. They also set the precedent for establishing covenants for a set period of time, usually at least twenty years, with automatic renewal clauses that establish the procedures for renewing or altering the covenants with the consent of at least a majority of the property owners (Urban Land Institute 1964).

The Early 1900s: Homeowners' Associations and Community Builders

The history of the initiation and diffusion of homeowners' associations is closely interconnected with the rise of community builders, such as Edward Bouton in Baltimore and J. C. Nichols in Kansas City, during the late 1800s and early 1900s. Community builders are real estate developers who design, engineer, finance, develop, and sell large-scale residential subdivisions. They recognized that homeowners' associations, such as the ones in Roland Park and Guilford, maximized the market appeal of large scale, fashionable residential developments by assuring prospective buyers that their neighborhood would not decline into higher density uses. The presence of a competent organization that would vigorously enforce deed restrictions, maintain common facilities, and provide needed services after all of the property in the division was sold and the developer had left the scene was a new and expedient means to protect property values and neighborhood aesthetics. The introduction of legally enforceable deed restrictions by community builders (now called CC&Rs—conditions, covenants, and restrictions) often went far beyond the scope of public sector regulations and constituted a significant abridgment of private property rights. In many cases these restrictions were eagerly accepted by affluent home buyers who desired stable and exclusive neighborhoods (Weiss and Watts 1989).

In 1905, the first massive, master-planned residential development in the United States utilizing homeowners' associations was started by J. C. Nichols in The Country Club District in Kansas City. A sixty-year project, Nichols began with a ten acre site just south of Kansas City. By 1964, The Country Club District encompassed over six thousand acres, twelve thousand homes, eleven major shopping centers, fifty thousand people, and twenty-nine districts, each with its own homeowners' association. Each of these associations is a separate corporation managed by a board of directors and elected by the residents of that district. The twenty-nine HOAs are linked together in a single federation, the Homes Association of Country Club District. Nine of the ten members of The Homes Association's board of directors are elected from among the authorized representatives of the twenty-nine homeowners' associations in the Country Club District and the tenth is selected by the J. C. Nichols Investment Company. The Homes Association's board of directors is responsible for providing all of the maintenance work for the entire District (Urban Land Institute 1964).

The Country Club District in Kansas City was modeled on the Roland Park subdivision with a few important modifications. In each of its twenty-nine districts, the J.C. Nichols Company organized the homeowners' association prior to the sale of the first lot and used self-perpetuating covenants that were automatically renewed after an initial term unless the owners of a majority of the front footage in the subdivision voted to amend or cancel them five years before the expiration date.

The Country Club District in Kansas City stands out not only as the largest residential development utilizing homeowners' associations during the early to mid-1900s but also as a source of inspiration for many other HOAs that were formed during the period. For example, several of the Country Club District's HOAs offered extensive recreational services, including golf courses, setting a precedent that is now a standard for many HOAs in larger subdivisions. The Homes Association of Country Club District also set the precedent for a more organized and tactful administrative style that was more effective in enforcing deed restrictions on a daily basis than an earlier reliance on lawsuits (Weiss and Watts 1989).

During the mid-1900s, the number of HOAs continued to increase in the United States primarily because the national government encouraged large-scale residential development through the policies of the Federal Housing Administration (FHA). Although the FHA did not specifically recommend the formation of residential community associations, it did promote the use of comprehensive deed restrictions and insisted that they be vigorously enforced. Reflecting the growing acceptance of HOAs, the Urban Land Institute formed a Community Builders' Council in 1944 with J.C. Nichols as its chairman. The Council strongly favored the use of HOAs and published a series of reports to assist developers in establishing HOAs on a sound basis. They advocated the immediate establishment of the HOA in the deed restrictions with company officials temporarily filling in as association directors until the resident directors were chosen, turning over control of the association to the homeowners in an orderly manner and as quickly as possible, delegating design control to an art jury (small committees of design professionals such as landscape architects, building architects, and civil engineers) rather than to the homeowners, and establishing recreational activities, including activities for children, as an important and integral function of the association (Weiss and Watts 1989).

The 1960s: Land Costs, PUDs, and the Condominium Boom

The 1960s marked a basic watershed in the history of RCAs. Although their numbers had continued to increase during the 1950s, there were still fewer than 1,000 RCAs in the United States in 1960 and most of them were homeowners' associations in relatively exclusive neighborhoods. At that time, the traditional residential subdivision with its minimum lot sizes, standard setback provisions for buildings, and wide public easements for streets and utilities began to be criticized for failing to provide developers an opportunity to respond in innovative ways to the increasingly scarce and expensive cost of land in urban and many suburban areas. As land became more expensive in these areas, the cost of housing increased to the point where many families could no longer afford to purchase a house. One solution employed by local governments to address the cost problem was to allow developers to increase the number of housing units they were allowed to build per acre. By constructing more homes per acre, the land cost per unit was reduced and the developer was able to offer the home at a more moderate price. Another solution was to relax regulatory standards concerning building setbacks, minimum lot sizes, street widths, and other infrastructure through the creation of planned unit developments (PUDs) (Dowden 1980).

PUDs (often referred to as cluster housing) allow developers to concentrate residential units on part of their property. To create a more suitable living environment for the residents, local governments typically require the developer to provide common open spaces and take greater care with preserving trees, rock outcroppings, and other natural features of the land. Because local governments did not want the financial responsibility for the maintenance and improvement of the open spaces, developers formed homeowners' associations to do the job (ACIR 1988).

PUDs came into their own during the 1960s. They allowed developers to offer a more marketable product to home buyers. The typical advertising for a PUD development touted the subdivision as "exclusive, maintenance free, country club living." Home buyers were attracted to PUDs because of their relatively moderate cost and the amenities they offered. Local government officials were attracted to them because they offered an opportunity to play a very active role in the design of the subdivision. Since the developer sought relaxation of the local government's subdivision regulations, local government's officials were in a strong position to negotiate assurances that the developer would meet certain standards and provide certain facilities and amenities.

At the same time PUDs were gaining widespread acceptance (causing the number of HOAs to accelerate), condominium sales soared, especially in California, Florida, and Hawaii (causing the number of COAs to accelerate). Condominiums offered consumers four distinct features that certain segments of the home-buying market viewed as advantages over the traditional single-family detached home. First, condominiums presented the consumer with a lower per-unit cost. Second, they relieved the consumer from the responsibility for exterior maintenance and upkeep. Third, they typically provided consumers more amenities and better recreational facilities because the cost of the amenities and facilities were shared with others in the condominium development. Finally, unlike most single family houses that were located in the suburbs and required a long commute to and from work, most condominiums were in urban areas, providing the home buyer with greater access to community amenities and services as well as a shorter commute (Dowden 1980).

As both PUDs and condominiums became more popular during the late 1960s and 1970s, the number of RCAs escalated exponentially, reaching 35,000 by 1980. This rapid growth was largely due to the expanded use of PUDs by local governments as a means of providing moderately priced housing and the growing market acceptance of condominiums, especially by older Americans who sought relief from yard and home maintenance and young families who desired the tax and investment benefits of home ownership but could not afford a single-family detached house. As indicated in Table 3.1, the U.S. Bureau of the Census started recording the number of condominium starts in 1970. At that time, condominiums accounted for approximately 9 percent of all new home construction. In 1973, condominiums increased their share of new

Table 3.1
Condominium Starts in the United States, Total Number and as a Percentage of All Housing Starts, 1970–1990

Year	*Total Number of Condominium Starts*	*Percent of All Housing Starts*
1990	150,000	13%
1988	148,000	10
1986	214,000	12
1984	291,000	16
1982	170,000	16
1980	186,000	14
1978	156,000	9
1976	95,000	6
1974	175,000	13
1972	212,000	9
1970	129,000	9

Sources: C. James Dowden. 1980. *Community Associations: A Guide for Public Officials.* Washington, DC: Urban Land Institute; U.S. Bureau of the Census. 1990. *Statistical Abstract of the United States, 1990.* Washington, DC: U.S. Government Printing Office; and U.S. Bureau of the Census. 1991. *Current Construction Reports, Housing Starts—February 1991.* Series C20–9102. Washington, DC: U.S. Government Printing Office.

home construction to 13 percent and that share has remained in the 10 to 16 percent range ever since (Dowden 1980).

The surge in condominium sales was also fueled by the national government's Housing Act of 1961. It substantially increased the availability of funds for the construction, sale, and resale of condominiums by making condominiums eligible for Federal Housing Administration mortgage insurance. The FHA also devised model-state enabling legislation to allow the conversion of apartments into condominiums and developed a method for standardizing the critical process of transferring control of RCAs from the developers to the homeowners. In projects with FHA-insured or Veteran's Administration guaranteed mortgages, the developers were required to retain at least a triple vote until 75 percent of the units were sold, at which point the developers formally relinquished majority voting control of the community association to the homeowners (Dowden 1986; Hyatt 1988).

The rapid spread of RCAs among more moderately priced housing and in smaller residential developments during the 1960s and early 1970s shifted the basic purposes of RCAs. Associations increasingly stressed the maintenance of common property and the provision of services, particularly recreational services, while the enforcement of deed restrictions to prevent neighborhood decline and protect the neighborhood's aesthetics became relatively less important (Weiss and Watts 1989).

The 1970s: Significant Growth Pains

Although several studies confirmed that during the 1970s most purchasers of homes governed by condominium or homeowners' associations were satisfied with their purchase, the rapid escalation in condominium and PUD development during the 1970s was accompanied by significant growth pains (Norcross 1973; U.S. Department of Housing and Urban Development 1975; Metropolitan Washington Council of Governments 1976). In many areas, especially in Florida, the mad dash to build condominiums created a flooded market that depressed sales prices and eroded consumer confidence in condominium resale values. Condominiums, in particular, were the subject of widespread ridicule in Florida's newspapers. Horror stories of shoddy workmanship and recreational facilities promised but never built were regular features. Many of these growth pains were a function of ignorance. Because condominiums were a fairly new form of real estate venture many developers were unfamiliar with the considerable complexities involved in managing them. Their attorneys, who drafted the association documents, had little or no prior experience with condominiums. Finding qualified and experienced management personnel to get the association off to a good operational start was often difficult if not impossible. Both state legislators who enacted enabling legislation for condominiums and local government officials who were approving and monitoring both condominium and PUD developments had only a vague outline of what to expect or what to be looking for. Moreover, most home buyers were abysmally ignorant regarding their roles as members of the association. As a result, much was done by trial and error, and there were many errors (Dowden 1980).

With the notable exception of condominium resale values, RCAs' problems during the 1970s usually fell within one of five problem areas. First, some developers took advantage of the flexibility they were given by local governments concerning design and construction standards and used inexpensive and inferior building materials and cut corners in other areas to maximize their profits. As one report put it: it is one thing to have a reduced right-of-way; it is something else to have a poorly constructed street without a proper pavement thickness (Longhini and Mosena 1978). Although it is fairly easy to blame these construction problems on unscrupulous developers, local government officials were also at fault. Primarily out of ignorance, most of them failed to negotiate strict design and construction standards during the project review process and later failed to monitor the developers' actions during the construction of the residential development.

A second problem area for RCAs during the 1970s dealt with finances. A large number of RCAs discovered after the developer had left the scene that the costs of maintaining private facilities and providing neighborhood services was far greater than anticipated. In some cases, homeowners charged that the developers had intentionally underestimated costs so they could advertise a deceptively low assessment fee to improve the marketability of the project. In other cases, developers openly subsidized the association's expenses during the initial stages of development, which led to misconceptions about the actual cost of running the association. As a result, many of the RCAs created during the 1970s had initial assessment fees that were set unrealistically low. These low assessment fees left many RCAs ill-prepared to take on the full responsibility for the association's financial obligations. To remedy the situation, RCA boards were forced to seek the permission of their membership to increase the association's assessment fee. Since many homeowners, particularly first-time home buyers, had stretched their personal finances to the limits to purchase their home, some RCAs were unable to secure permission to raise the assessment fees. As a result, they were forced to either dip into the association's capital reserves, reduce services, or delay maintenance. Compounding the financial problem was that most RCA documents at the time limited annual assessment fee increases to 5 percent a year; a figure that was often too low to keep up with the relatively high rates of inflation during the 1970s and far too low to deal with unexpected repair costs to high-cost items such as sewer and water lines (Longhini and Mosena 1978).

Another problem area for RCAs during the 1970s was consumer misunderstanding. A survey of local planning officials in 1973 revealed that 50 percent of them believed that home buyers did not fully understand the responsibilities of living in a RCA-governed community. Most local and state governments at the time did not require the developer to explain the costs and responsibilities of association membership to prospective buyers. In the few states and localities that did require disclosure, relatively few home buyers actually read the material. Surveys of RCA members revealed that most were unaware that their association had a reserve account or that they owned the development's streets (Longhini and Mosena 1978).

The fourth problem area for RCAs during the 1970s dealt with management. Because many RCA members did not fully understand the responsibilities of association membership, relatively few of them became actively involved in association management and the few who did generally had little or no professional management training. Very few home buyers were aware that their association was required to prepare an annual budget and income tax return, was subject to an annual audit, had to supervise all maintenance activities, represent the association at public hearings, implement social programs, hire contractors, and provide for insurance. Nearly half of the planners responding to the 1973 survey felt that the RCA board members that they dealt with lacked the necessary knowledge and experience to run an effective RCA (Longhini and Mosena 1978).

A fifth problem for RCAs during the 1970s was phasing. Many of the larger residential developments during this period were built in phases, usually covering four to five years. Often, the developer built the subdivision's amenities and recreational facilities during the first phase of the development. This created a dangerous situation where a relatively small number of homes in the early development phases carried the financial burden of amenities and recreational facilities designed for a much larger number of homes. If the sales of units in future phases were brisk, then the existing homeowners did not experience a long-term financial problem. However, in some cases future sales were slow and, in a few cases, the developer went bankrupt, leaving the first homeowners with a heavy financial burden. Another phasing problem arose from the opposite cause, where home buyers in the development's early phases were promised amenities, such as a golf course or tennis courts, that were never completed or were delayed for years beyond the original estimated time of completion. Thirty percent of the local planning officials responding to the 1973 survey indicated that they knew of at least one development in their community that had failed to complete all its housing units and 42 percent of them reported that there was at least one development in their community that had not completed all its promised amenities (Longhini and Mosena 1978).

Recognizing that a growing dissatisfaction existed with RCA performance and that this dissatisfaction was affecting sales, developers and builders (through the Urban Land Institute and the National Association of Home Builders) formed the independent and nonprofit Community Associations Institute (CAI) in 1973. CAI's mission was to promote the establishment of community associations by providing developers, managers, and homeowners with educational material on how to form and operate successful community associations. Since its inception CAI has published numerous pamphlets establishing guidelines for all aspects of community association life, including the association's creation, its management, finances, and internal governance procedures. It has also held numerous workshops and technical programs for developers, association managers, and association members (Weiss and Watts 1989).

By the end of the 1970s, most of the major problems with condominium and PUD developments that stemmed from ignorance had been corrected. As one report noted in 1980, builders, lawyers, managers, and the buying public had become much more aware of how condominiums and PUDs could be structured to prevent the abuses and problems that occurred at the outset of the decade. Moreover, the various state legislatures had taken steps to prevent the most blatant abuses that had occurred in the past. Although there were still problems to be worked out, it was clear by the early 1980s that PUDs and condominiums were maturing as real estate ventures (Dowden 1980).

The 1980s: Economics and Lifestyles Fuel Continued RCA Growth

During the 1980s nearly 100,000 additional RCAs were formed, bringing the total by the end of the decade to over 130,000. Much of this growth was in relatively small residential projects, often infill development in established neighborhoods. The rapid acceleration in the number of RCAs was caused primarily by the continued market demand for alternatives to the traditional single-family tract home and by developers responding to changes in local government's subdivision regulations. Facing fiscal difficulties, many local governments during the 1980s began to require developers of new homes to assume increased financial responsibility for streets, sewers, and other infrastructure costs. Because the infrastructure costs of existing homes had been subsidized by local government, developers of new homes faced the prospect of being priced out of the local housing market. In an effort to market competitively priced housing, developers of new homes often sought exemptions from local building standards and regulations. Because many local governments were reluctant to grant these exemptions, developers increasingly turned to PUDs and condominiums as a means to reduce development expenses, market competitively priced homes, and, at the same time, insure an adequate return on their investment (Weiss and Watts 1989).

The trend toward smaller RCAs during the 1980s altered the emphasis for RCA development. Prior to the 1970s, the enforcement of the neighborhood's deed restrictions or covenants was primarily viewed by consumers as RCAs' most redeeming feature. During the 1970s, RCAs' role in protecting property values became a secondary concern for most consumers. Instead, they were buying into PUD and condominium developments primarily because they offered home buyers a maintenance-free lifestyle coupled with extensive recreational facilities. During the 1980s, the protection of property values and the provision of an alternative lifestyle continued to attract buyers to PUDs and condominiums, but developers also discovered that the rapidly escalating cost of single-family homes, particularly on the east and west coasts, played an increasingly important role in the consumers' decision to purchase a home in a PUD or condominium development.

Recognizing that the demand for PUDs and condominiums was increasing among less affluent, often first-time home buyers, many of the RCAs formed during the 1980s offered fewer amenities and services than those formed during the previous two decades. By offering fewer services, developers were able to keep association fees low enough to attract these new buyers (Weiss and Watts 1989). As a result, by the end of the decade the stereotype of condominiums being enclaves for either the elderly or for young, swinging singles and of HOAs being exclusive resorts for the very rich no longer applied. RCA residents had become quite diverse, covering all income levels and age groups. Moreover, the proliferation of RCA communities had also made it nearly impossible to stereotype RCAs. They now ranged in size and responsibilities from a few homes on a single street that collectively provide only one or two services to thousands of homes comprising a mid-size city such as Reston, Virginia, that offer dozens of services (Barton and Silverman 1987a).

In terms of RCAs' historical development, the 1980s will be recognized both for the rapid escalation in the number of RCAs and for attempts by developers and others to establish standardized RCA management techniques. As one report noted at the outset of the 1980s, many of the initial problems resulting from the formation of condominium and PUD developments had been overcome during the 1970s, but the one concern that still stood out as a problem was the management and operation of both condominium and homeowners' associations once the developer had left the scene (Dowden 1980).

Among the new management practices established during the 1980s was a revision in the timing of the transition period from developer to homeowner control of the association. In many cases, developers began to relinquish control of the association after 50 percent of the homes had been sold as opposed to the standard 75 percent benchmark. This resulted primarily from court decisions that held developers legally liable for failing to budget adequately, collect assessments, or provide promised amenities. By relinquishing control to the homeowners, the association's board of directors assumed this liability. The CAI also played a key role in this area by giving developers detailed, step-by-step models for transferring control of the association to the homeowners (Weiss and Watts 1989).

Another management area that received much attention during the 1980s was the initial resources made available to associations following the transition period. Surveys of RCA board members during the 1980s reported that developers were becoming much more responsible by setting initial assessment fees at levels that were adequate for financing the association once the developer had left the scene. This improvement was largely attributed to CAI's educational efforts and by increased regulatory efforts in this area by local governments (Barton and Silverman 1987a).

The 1990s: Continued Growth and a Different Set of Questions

Most of the problems that appeared during the 1970s concerning PUD and condominium developments' formation and transition periods have been solved. The current emphasis is on improving the management of RCAs after the developer has left the scene. There is universal agreement that during the 1980s RCA management improved among the larger RCAs, thanks in large part to CAI's educational efforts and the improvement of operational procedures through trial and error. However, problems do remain. Areas of concern include the continuing problem of developers leaving behind uncorrected major construction defects that subsequently threaten the financial stability of the association following the transition period, the lack of financial reserve studies or established preventive maintenance programs, and inadequate preparation of resident board members, particularly among the smaller RCAs. A study of California RCAs conducted in 1986 found that in many cases, board members in smaller RCAs do not recognize the legal liabilities of serving on the board and in many instances do not keep records of their actions or minutes of their meetings (Barton and Silverman 1987a).

The proliferation of smaller RCAs during the 1980s presents a new set of problems for RCA residents. Because most of the smaller RCAs are self-managed, their board members are the ones most in need of objective, professional advice concerning the management of their association. The best source of information on running successful RCAs is the Community Association Institute. However, most small RCAs are not members of CAI and do not receive its publications. As a result, most RCAs are run by individuals who often mean well but generally do not know what they are doing or where to turn to for help. Addressing their needs will be a priority for RCA advocates during the remainder of the 1990s and beyond.

RCAs are no longer considered innovative new entries in the housing market. They are an accepted and widespread form of housing occupied by over thirty million Americans. Market demand for PUDs and condominiums continues to be strong, particularly in the expensive housing markets on the east and west coasts, developers continue to view them as profitable economic ventures, and local governments continue to regard them as convenient devices to subsidize their infrastructure and service delivery expenses. As a result, the debate at city council and county government meetings during the 1990s and beyond is not going to be whether new RCAs should be established. The number of RCAs in the United States will continue to increase exponentially. However, for the past twenty years the debate over the desirability of PUDs and condominiums has focused primarily on the issues of housing marketability, developer profitability, and local government's budgetary considerations. Little attention has been paid to the impact PUD and condominium developments have on the delivery of public services, local political relationships and issues, or American governance. These considerations are certain to play a more prominent role in the debate over the desirability of PUDs and condominiums in the years ahead and are discussed in detail in the following chapters.

4

The Privatization of Public Services: The Theoretical Arguments

Reflecting the growing importance of RCAs in American life, the nation's leading newspapers increased the amount of space devoted to RCA activities throughout the 1980s. A computer search of the *New York Times, Los Angeles Times, Christian Science Monitor, Wall Street Journal,* and *Washington Post* revealed that during the 1980s sixty articles concerning RCAs appeared. During this period, the number of articles featuring RCAs increased each year, reaching a high of sixteen in 1989. Although some articles dealt with RCAs' efforts to alter local development and zoning decisions, most concerned lawsuits filed by homeowners who were unhappy with their RCA's enforcement of the neighborhood's CC&Rs and were willing to commit an inordinate amount of time, effort, and money to defend their right to do whatever they wanted with their property. For example, in Newport Beach, California, a homeowner spent over $10,000 in an eight-year legal battle with her RCA in an effort to keep the family's basketball hoop over their garage door. She finally won an out-of-court settlement. In Palos Verdes, California, a homeowner refused to pay his $1,165 annual assessment fee because he claimed that his RCA's gardener had used illegal pesticides that resulted in the death of his two goldfish. The RCA sued the homeowner for not paying the assessment fee and, after lengthy legal wrangling, the California courts ordered the homeowner to pay the association the $1,165 assessment fee plus $44,064 to cover the association's attorney fees and court costs. When the homeowner's attorney fees were included, his total bill came to over $58,000—or $29,000 for each goldfish (Klein 1988; Miller 1990).

Newspaper coverage of legal disputes among RCA members trivializes the important role RCAs play in American governance. For millions of Americans, RCAs have become a governing entity that is as important to them as their town or city government. Like the public sector, RCAs provide goods and services and have the power to tax residents to pay for them. In addition, like the public sector's policing powers, RCAs regulate their residents' behavior. Moreover, like the public sector, RCAs have elective institutions based on republican principles that determine such issues as what is considered appropriate behavior in the neighborhood, what the punishments will be for those violating those norms and what type and level of services will be provided in the neighborhood.

As mentioned in Chapter 3, the number of RCAs in the United States is expected to continue to grow exponentially. One of the more important factors responsible for this growth is that many local government officials now view PUD and condominium developments as the only viable housing alternative available because they recognize that they do not have the financial resources available to provide the infrastructure necessary to make the project feasible. They also recognize that they do not have the financial resources to provide services to the neighborhood's residents once they have moved into their homes. While some capital-intensive public services, such as wastewater purification and disposal, have economies of scale that are beyond the resources of most RCAs, local governments can, and do, realize substantial savings by transferring many of their infrastructure costs and service delivery responsibilities to RCAs. As a result, unless housing preferences change dramatically, the number of RCAs will continue their rapid growth for the rest of this decade and well into the twenty-first century. Moreover, as their numbers increase, RCAs will continue to shift a portion of what is currently considered public responsibilities and politics into a private framework. As a recent report by the U.S. Advisory Commission on Intergovernmental Relations indicated, RCAs account for the most significant privatization of local government responsibilities in recent times (ACIR 1989). Surprisingly, the literature on privatization rarely mentions RCAs or their role in providing public services. For example, the most recent book by one of the nation's foremost advocates of privatization devotes less than one page of coverage to RCAs. However, that author did argue that RCAs should be encouraged because they provide a "desperately needed sense of community" and "can restore citizenship skills atrophied from disuse, skills without which a democracy cannot long survive" (Savas 1987).

The privatization literature touches upon one of the most fundamental questions of American governance: Who should decide. As mentioned in Chapter 1, most discussions of public policies center on the question, "What should we do?" For example, it is not uncommon to hear policymakers and lobbyists asking if we (meaning government) should guarantee the poor a minimum income, provide subsidies to farmers, or build mass transit systems instead of interstate highways. But before asking the "what should we do" question, we must examine the assumption that government is the most appropriate mechanism for providing goods and services or for regulating economic and social interactions. Specifically, it is necessary to ask the "who should decide" question. Should the decision to provide specific goods and services or to regulate specific economic and social interactions be left to government or to the economic law of supply and demand in the private marketplace. If government makes the decision, should the national government, the state governments, or the local governments decide? Moreover, if there is evidence to suggest that either the private marketplace, churches, charities, or volunteers can provide specific types of goods and services more efficiently and effectively than government, should they be allowed or encouraged to provide them? If not, why not? If neighbors formed into residential community associations can supply specific types of goods and services more efficiently and effectively than their local government, should they be allowed or encouraged to provide them? If not, why not?

Precedent suggests that the answer to the question of "who should decide?" will influence the answer to the question of "what should we do?" (Henig 1985). Therefore, it is important to carefully examine the arguments presented by those who advocate one level of government as opposed to another and by those who advocate an emphasis on the private sector versus those who advocate an emphasis on the public sector. It is also important to examine the performance of the public sector, the private sector, and entities such as RCAs that share attributes of both before deciding the appropriate response to the question of "who should decide?"

This chapter presents a historical overview of the public sector's role in the United States. It also gives the various arguments surrounding the question of "who shall decide"—specifically, the arguments of those who advocate the growth of the public sector and those who oppose it. In addition, the debate among the public sector's advocates concerning whether the national, state, or local governments should be given the most authority is also examined. Finally, it presents the arguments of those who advocate the privatization of specific types of goods and services. The role of RCAs in providing public goods and services and as a part of the privatization movement is examined in Chapter 5.

The Growth of the Public Sector

Prior to the economic depression of the 1930s, the answer to the "who shall decide" question was rarely government. Instead, depending on the specific issue involved, the answer was usually the private marketplace, the churches, charities, or volunteers. The public sector was viewed as an actor of last resort for a variety of reasons, including, but not limited to, public complacency, apathy and ignorance concerning the plight of the poor and the existence of economic and social discrimination against minorities, sectional antagonisms that hindered national government activism, particularly in Congress, and parochial viewpoints that generally precluded the consideration of governmental activism. Moreover, the American political culture at that time was dominated by a negative liberal tradition that identified individual liberty as freedom from governmental coercion and constraint (Hartz 1955). The view that liberty was synonymous with freedom from governmental action meshed nicely with the prevailing classical economic doctrine of laissez faire, where individuals must be free of governmental restraints to enable them to reach maximum efficiency and productivity in the marketplace. As a result, government's appropriate role was generally viewed as being limited to protecting life and property and enforcing contracts (Burns et al. 1990). As Thomas Jefferson put it: government is best which governs least (Conlan 1981b).

America's negative liberal tradition fit the needs of a rural, segmented society where most individuals were self-sufficient farmers and most others lived in relatively small, autonomous towns that had relatively few and inconsequential economic and social ties to other towns in their state. However, as the American economy industrialized, individuals began to leave the farms for manufacturing or service-related jobs in newly formed and growing cities. Americans became increasingly interdependent as industrialization's specialization and division of labor caused them to depend upon others to grow their food, build their shelters, and provide their clothing and other necessities of life. Moreover, technological advances in communications and transportation systems made intercity and interstate trade feasible. As trade increased, America's rising standard of living became increasingly dependent upon the many and substantial economic ties among its cities and states (Beer 1974).

As the industrial revolution altered the social and economic fabric of American society, piecemeal efforts occurred to involve government in the regulation of business affairs, especially the regulation of trusts, railroads, interstate commerce, and wages and working conditions. There were also efforts to subsidize economic development through public works projects and to provide programs to care for those deemed to be unemployable. However, the prevailing faith in laissez-faire macroeconomics, coupled with the influence of local values and constitutional interpretations, helped confine most of the demands and responses for governmental involvement prior to the Great Depression to the state and local levels (Conlan 1981b).

As the industrial revolution progressed and economic wealth began to flow into the hands of a relatively few families that controlled several large industrial enterprises, the tenets of negative liberalism began to be attacked by leading members of the professional middle class (primarily academics, attorneys, and doctors) who called themselves the Progressives. In their view, the concentration of wealth in the hands of a relatively few families constituted a far greater threat to personal liberty than government ever did. They were convinced that the wealthy were using their economic clout to systematically eliminate competition in the marketplace. They were also "investing" a portion of their wealth in the political process, buying both access and favors from corrupt politicians and the party bosses who were largely responsible for putting the corrupt politicians into elective office. The goal of these investments was to ensure that government did not obstruct their attempts to reach monopoly status. The Progressives were convinced that the concentration of wealth into a relatively few families made government intervention in the marketplace necessary to ensure fair competition and prevent the emergence of economic monopolies that could set prices at will instead of according to the economic laws of supply and demand. To achieve this goal, they advocated governmental reforms, such as the initiative, referendum, and recall and the imposition of civil service systems, to weaken the influence of corrupt party bosses and politicians who may have been elected by the people but were not, in their view, representing the public's interest. They were convinced that only an "honest" government could regulate these powerful economic forces that were far beyond any individual's control.

The Progressives received a great deal of media attention during the early 1900s and were able to achieve some governmental reforms aimed at weakening the party system's political bosses. They were also responsible, at least in part, for the adoption of state and national legislation that regulated the economic power of certain trusts. However, for the most part, the public continued to view government as an actor of last resort. It was only after it had become obvious that the private market—the churches, charities, and volunteers—could not cope with the economic devastation of the Great Depression and the social problems caused by unemployment rates that peaked at nearly 33 percent, that the answer to the "who shall decide" question began to shift decidedly toward the public sector.

As the role of the public sector in providing goods and services and in regulating economic activity increased to meet the social and economic needs created by the Great Depression, individuals and businesses that felt they were adversely affected by government's actions turned to the courts for relief. At first, the U.S. Supreme Court's decisions tended to restrain the scope of the public sector's activities. But following President Franklin Roosevelt's advocacy of the Court Bill of 1937 which would have expanded the size of the Supreme Court to fifteen, enough to give advocates of the public sector a majority on the court, the U.S. Supreme Court altered its course and, in general, its constitutional interpretations no longer prohibited the growth of the public sector. However, the U.S. Constitution only specified that governmental power was to be shared between the states and the national government. It was ambiguous concerning what those powers were and how they were to be shared (Colella 1986, Dilger 1986). As a result, the "who shall decide" question was generally replaced in the courts, in the halls of Congress, and in academia by the question of "which governmental body shall decide": the national government, the state governments, the local governments, or a combination of all three governments.

Since the Great Depression, the U.S. Supreme Court has been asked in nearly every court session to determine the appropriate balance of power between the national government and the states and localities in one sphere of activity or another. Although the Supreme Court's rulings have not always been one sided, with a series of ups and downs for the national government, the Court has generally discounted the importance of the Tenth Amendment's protection of states' rights and has upheld the national government's authority to preempt state actions in a number of different spheres, including the authority to regulate economic production [*National Labor Relations Board v. Jones and Laughlin Steel Corporation* (1937)]; commerce [*Garcia v. San Antonio Metropolitan Transit Authority* (1985)]; social relations [*Brown v. Board of Education, Topeka, Kansas* (1954/55)]; and to tax and spend for the general welfare [*Steward Machine Company v. Davis* (1937), *South Dakota v. Dole* (1987), *South Carolina v. Baker* (1988)] (Colella 1981; Howard 1986; Hunter and Oakerson 1986; Wrightson 1989; and Hickok 1990). In fact, from 1936 to 1976, the U.S. Supreme Court did not overturn a single act of Congress for encroaching unduly upon the powers of the states. In 1976, the Supreme Court ruled in *National League of Cities v. Usery* that the Tenth Amendment placed limits on the national government's commerce power as it applied to state and local governments. As a result, the Supreme Court ruled that Congress lacked the authority to regulate the wages and hours of state and local government employees engaged in what the Supreme Court labeled as traditional government functions. However, the Court subsequently changed its mind in *Garcia v. San Antonio Metropolitan Transit Authority* (1985) when it ruled that states had to look to the political process and not to the courts and interpretations of the Tenth Amendment for protection against what the states viewed as obtrusive and unconstitutional actions by the national government. As a result, the Supreme Court overturned *National League of Cities v. Usery* and ruled that the national government's commerce power did allow it to regulate the wages and hours of state and local government employees, even if they were engaged in what the Supreme Court had previously labeled as being a traditional government function (Hunter and Oakerson 1986; Howard 1986; Hickok 1990).

At the same time that the courts "got out of the way of the national government," the American political culture continued to evolve in a manner that was more generally supportive of an expanded role for the public sector in decisionmaking and especially for the national government. Although the traditional values of individual initiative, private enterprise, and limited, localized government were still valued by most Americans, they also accepted the basic elements of the welfare state, where the national government was viewed as having the primary responsibility for ensuring a minimally decent standard of living for the "worthy" poor: the elderly, handicapped, orphans, and anyone else who was unable to care for themselves (Conlan 1981b). Most Americans had also accepted the notion that government expansion was an inevitable response to the failures of unregulated private markets (Henig 1990).

As the constitutional and cultural restraints to national government activism fell to the wayside, the only remaining obstacles to the national government's expansion was the existence of the conservative coalition in Congress, Congress' institutional rules, such as the seniority system, which favored southern conservatives, and the lack of a strong commitment to government activism by the President of the United States. The congressional and presidential elections of 1964 eliminated the first and third restraints as large Democratic majorities were elected to the Congress and Lyndon Johnson was elected President. With Johnson's encouragement, Congress approved a flood of legislation during the mid-1960s collectively designed to create what the Johnson Administration called a "Great Society." At the same time, the legislation moved the national government to the forefront of many activities, including, but not limited to, civil rights, health care, consumer protection, and pollution control—all areas previously viewed as state or local functions (Conlan 1981b).

As the public grew more accustomed to the national government's activism, debate in the halls of Congress began to focus on the cost and effectiveness of the national government's programs, not whether they should exist. As James Q. Wilson commented in 1979:

> Until very recently, the chief issue in any congressional argument over new policies was whether it was legitimate for the federal government to do something at all. . . . But once the initial law is passed, the issue of legitimacy disappears.

The trend toward centralizing decisionmaking authority in the national government was slowed following Ronald Reagan's election to the presidency in 1980. At that time, the national economy was in recession; the consumer price index was rising at a rate of 13 percent a year; the unemployment rate was 7 percent and rising; the national government's annual deficit had reached record levels; the continuing energy crisis promised to lower the nation's standard of living; the American dollar was being replaced by the Japanese yen as the world's dominant currency; for the first time in memory, many products produced in other countries, especially automobiles and electronics, were universally recognized as being of a higher quality than domestic made products; and several members of Congress had recently been indicted for seeking or accepting bribes. Not surprisingly, cynicism and disillusionment with the national government's performance had reached record levels. The University of Michigan's Institute for Social Research, which had been charting the public's attitudes toward government since 1958, reported that only 19 percent of the nation exhibited trusting opinions concerning the national government in 1978, a record low. In addition, 52 percent exhibited cynical attitudes toward the national government, a record high (Harwood 1980).

This popular frustration with the national government's lack of effectiveness, coupled with new public choice theories that suggested that the public sector was inherently inefficient and new academic findings that suggested that state and local governments had dramatically improved their capacity to govern, produced a broad gauged backlash against both centralized government and activist government at all levels (Salamon 1989). This backlash was epitomized by President Reagan's New Federalism proposals in 1981 and 1982 designed to both decentralize domestic public policy authority from the national government to the state governments and decrease the overall influence of the public sector in domestic public policy (Conlan and Walker 1983; Williamson 1986; Conlan 1988).

Many of President Reagan's New Federalism's proposals were not adopted and many others were modified. As a result, massive shifts in governmental authority did not take place, but the trends toward enhancing the public sector's role in decisionmaking and in centralizing authority in the national government were slowed and those who would answer the question of "who should decide" with a firm response of "the national government" were put on the defensive (Williamson 1990).

The Argument for the Public Sector

Economists have suggested that there are four basic types of goods and services: private, toll, common pool, and collective. They are distinguished by the way they are consumed (individually or collectively) and by the relative difficulty in preventing their consumption without payment (easy or difficult). Private goods and services, such as clothing, are individually consumed and it is relatively easy to prevent their consumption without payment. Common pool goods and services, such as air, water, and wild animals, occur naturally and are individually consumed. However, it is relatively difficult to prevent the consumption of common pool goods and services without payment. Toll goods and services, such as electricity, are collectively consumed and it is relatively easy to prevent their consumption without payment. Collective goods and services, such as national defense, police protection, and immunization, are collectively consumed or have benefits that are collectively shared. However, it is relatively difficult to prevent their consumption or their enjoyment without payment (Savas 1987).

Most economists, even those who advocate a minimal role for the public sector in decisionmaking, agree that the private marketplace is not capable of maintaining an adequate supply of common pool and collective goods and services because it is very difficult for suppliers to prevent them from being consumed for free. Under such circumstances, every individual has an incentive to become a "free rider" and make full use of the goods and services without paying for them. This generally results in the overconsumption of common pool goods. For example, many wild animals have been hunted to the point of extinction because the demand for their meat or their hides far exceeded their supply. Since the supply of wild animals is relatively fixed by nature, increasing the price of their meat or their hides did not have a large impact on its supply. The only way to prevent the demand for common pool goods from overwhelming their supply is for the public sector to regulate their consumption.

Government interference in the private marketplace is also appropriate for collective goods and services but the problem is not their consumption. Instead, the problem is the reluctance of private suppliers to produce the good or provide the service. Since consumers are reluctant to pay for collective goods and services, such as police protection or national defense, suppliers in the private marketplace are reluctant to produce them. Therefore, collective contributions, usually through government-imposed taxes and user fees, are necessary to assure an adequate supply of collective goods (Savas 1987).

Advocates of an enhanced role for the public sector in decision-making go beyond the efficiency arguments presented by economists by arguing that many goods and services, such as education, mass transit, and food, are so worthy that their consumption should be encouraged even though they are not subject to the free-rider problem. In their view, government's role is not limited to perfecting the failures of the private marketplace in an attempt to achieve an efficient society. Instead, they believe that government's role is to promote a more equitable and just society. As a result, government should supply worthy goods and services to consumers regardless of their ability or willingness to pay. As a result, they advocate government policies that either subsidize the production of worthy goods and services or have the government produce these goods and services directly and supply it to those who are considered needy (Savas 1987).

Those who advocate an enhanced role for the public sector also tend to advocate Keynesian economics. Keynesians believe that government is a necessary mechanism for stabilizing the business cycle. They argue that during recessions businesses tend to reduce production and lay off workers to cope with weakened demand for their products. As more people are laid off, demand for goods and services weakens further because people have less money to spend. As demand falls, businesses continue to lay off workers and a vicious downward economic slide ensues that can lead to a depression. To prevent this, Keynesians argue that the national government should step in during these economic downturns and increase the demand for goods and services by increasing government spending, even if it means incurring a deficit. Keynesians are convinced that the demand for goods and services will increase because the additional government spending will increase the amount of disposable income in the economy. As the increased demand for goods and services reduces business' inventories, businesses will recall laid off workers, increase the working hours of current employees, hire additional employees, or a combination of these actions to replenish their inventories. As a result, the national economy's decline will be halted and, if the government's spending stimulus is applied appropriately, the national economy will grow and produce the necessary conditions for continued economic growth (Gordon 1984; McConnell 1984).

Advocates of enhancing the public sector's role in decisionmaking also tend to view government as the only viable mechanism for redistributing wealth in society. This is accomplished by establishing progressive revenue systems and expenditure patterns that direct a disproportionate amount of government revenue to the poor and working class. By redistributing income to these groups, economic growth is assured because their demand for goods and services remains at a level necessary to sustain the economy. The redistribution of income also serves the ideological goal of enhancing the economic position of the poor and the working class. Finally, they also argue that government regulation of business is necessary to protect consumers from avaricious business practices.

The Argument for the Private Sector

Advocates of a greater reliance on the private sector in decisionmaking argue that it is appropriate for the public sector to perfect the imperfections of the marketplace by regulating the consumption of common pool goods and assisting the private sector in supplying collective goods. However, when prices are capable of ensuring a balance between the supply and the demand for a good or service, the government's role should be limited to preventing cheating by taking actions such as enforcing contracts and assuring product safety (Savas 1987).

Those who advocate a greater reliance on the private sector in decisionmaking also disagree strongly with Keynesian economic thought, do not share the ideological goal of redistributing wealth, and question the need for government regulation of business. They argue that the American economy has not kept pace with economic growth in other nations, particularly Japan, because Keynesian macroeconomic policies have resulted in huge government deficits. To finance these deficits, government must compete with private firms for available capital. As the demand for capital increases, so does its price (interest rates). As interest rates rise, so do the costs of investment. As investment costs rise, private firms restrict their economic ventures which, in turn, inhibits economic growth. Moreover, although government spending during economic downturns does increase demand for goods and services, much of that demand is for goods produced in other countries, such as automobiles and electronics produced by Japanese companies. As a result, increasing government spending during economic downturns does not stimulate the American domestic economy very much, but it does contribute greatly to the accumulation of government deficits. Therefore, instead of using government expenditures to even out the business cycle, they advocate either monetarism (the money supply should be kept at a constant rate to prevent alternate economic booms and busts), neoclassical (the national government should play a very passive role in regulating the economy), or supply-side economic theories (the national government should increase the supply of goods and services in the economy by reducing marginal income tax rates so that people will have an incentive to work and invest more).

Advocates of the private sector also believe that government regulation of business practices inhibits economic growth because that intervention often results in higher production costs. Also, special economic interests often "capture" a government agency and use their influence to get the agency to wield its authority not to protect the consumer's interests but restrict competition (Friedman 1979).

Advocates of the private sector also disagree strongly with the ideological goal of redistributing wealth. They believe in equality of opportunity, not equality of outcome. In their view, individuals are born with different talents and abilities and should be provided an opportunity to be rewarded in the economic marketplace based on their performance. Government's role is to prevent individuals from facing arbitrary obstacles that may prevent them from using their capabilities to pursue their own objectives. As a result, government should halt any practices that deny individuals access to positions for which they are qualified because of their ethnic background, color, gender, or religion. However, government should not endeavor to redistribute income because it reduces the individual's incentive to maximize productivity. When given the proper incentives, individuals will add wealth to the community as a whole that is many times greater than the wealth accumulated by the innovators (Friedman 1979). As the old saying goes, "a rising tide raises all ships."

Those who advocate an emphasis on the private sector also believe that economic freedom is an essential requisite for political freedom. As Milton Friedman has written, the combination of economic and political power in the same hands is a sure recipe for tyranny (Friedman 1979).

The Centralization/Decentralization Debate

Advocates of enhancing the public sector's role in decisionmaking disagree over the appropriate distribution of authority among the national, state, and local governments. Those who advocate the centralization of governmental power have argued that the national government must take the lead in public policy primarily because state and local governments cannot be trusted with power. They have argued that although state and local government officials have from time to time been innovative, efficient, and progressive in racial and economic affairs, in general, they lack expertise, tend to be narrow-mined and parochial, and are structurally incapable of engaging in policies that redistribute from the rich to the poor (Henig 1985). Moreover, because the national government's fiscal resources are superior to those of the states and localities, only it can ensure uniform levels of essential services throughout the nation, especially since state and local governments' fiscal capacities vary so much (ACIR 1978). In addition, state and local governments are often unable to levy sufficient taxes to provide sufficient services because they compete among themselves for business investment and taxpaying residents. The national government's revenue system is also more efficient and progressive than most state and local government's revenue systems and should be used as a means of providing general support (Barfield 1981).

Advocates of enhancing the national government's authority also argue that there are certain fundamental goals, such as civil rights, equal employment opportunities, and care for the poor and aged that can only be achieved by the national government because it is difficult to achieve change when reform-minded citizens must deal with 50 state governments and nearly 80,000 local governments. In addition, the national government has the right and the obligation to offer programs that encourage state and local governments to demonstrate new approaches to solving domestic policy problems. For example, national grants have provided seed money as the first step toward the development of larger, full-scale programs in such areas as mass transit, juvenile delinquency, and prenatal care (Barfield 1981). Finally, there are some governmental services with either costs or benefits that spill over onto other localities or states. For example, water and air pollution controls benefit not only the local community that pays for those controls, but all the communities that are located downwind or downstream from that community. Since state and local taxpayers are generally reluctant to pay for programs whose benefits go to others, state and local governments often do not adequately finance programs with significant spillover effects. As a result, the national government should step in to ensure that these programs are funded at their optimum levels (Dilger 1989).

The Argument for Decentralization

Reflecting a general dissatisfaction with the performance of the national government, the trend toward centralization of governmental power has slowed since the early 1980s. Opponents of centralization tend to fall into two categories, those who advocate decentralization and those who advocate privatization. Decentralization calls for shrinking the scope of governmental activities by putting greater authority in the hands of state and local governments. Privatization goes farther. Its advocates suggest that governmental authority should be reduced altogether, not simply shifted among the three levels of government.

Advocates of decentralization argue that state and local governments can and should be trusted with power. They point to James Madison's arguments in *The Federalist Papers* which defend federalism as one of several checks and balances necessary to prevent governmental tyranny and as an effective device to recognize and protect the diversity of values and opinions held by territorially defined groups (Conlan 1981a). In their view, concentrations of governmental power should be avoided to safeguard individual and local liberties (Elazar 1968). As one decentralization advocate has written,

> It is as dangerous to conduct a representative democracy under monolithic central authority as it is to drive a car without brakes down the highway. Restraint mechanisms are highly recommended (Williamson 1990).

Advocates of decentralization also point to rational choice theories that justify decentralization as the best organizational solution to meet regional variations in preferences for public goods and services. Rather than having the central government produce a uniform level of public goods and services that consumers will consider too high in some areas and too low in others, decentralization allows each jurisdiction to respond to local preferences more precisely. As a result, decentralization increases government efficiency by providing a range of outputs that corresponds more closely to the differing tastes of various consumer groups (Oates 1972).

Decentralization's advocates dismiss the centralists' argument that state and local governments lack the capacity to govern well. They note that changes in population have made the states and localities more competent and more sensitive to urban needs, that states and localities have reformed their taxing structures to render them more flexible and progressive, and that legal systems have been reformed to ensure that states and localities are more responsive to the interests of minorities and the poor (Henig 1985). Moreover, political reforms have brought about structural changes that make state and local governments more effective, professional, and responsive to citizen's needs (Bowman and Kearney 1986). For example, nearly all the states have revised their state constitutions since 1955 in ways that conform more closely to the general principles of brevity, simplicity, lack of encumbering restraints, and a reasonable process for amendment or revision (ACIR 1985). State legislatures have also been reformed and upgraded. Among other changes, many states have adopted annual legislative sessions, single-member districts, unlimited legislative sessions, and presession organization; reduced the number of committees and committee assignments; adopted uniform legislative rules; required committee meeting notices; and increased professional staff and informational services (Reeves 1990). The governors' capacity to govern has also been improved. Their tenure in office has been increased to allow more time for implementing programs and their formal powers have been increased. Forty-four governors now have line-item veto power and many states have strengthened the governors' authority over the states' budgetary processes (Reeves 1990). Governors also now have a broader range of institutions and systems, as evidenced by larger staffs and the relocation of state policy-planning offices into the governor's office, to assist them in their administrative and policymaking efforts than most of their predecessors (Beyle 1988).

Finally, advocates of decentralization argue that active state and local governments promote a sense of state and community responsibility and self-reliance, that state and local governments are closer to the people and better able to adapt public programs to state and local needs and conditions, that they encourage participation and civic responsibility by allowing more people to become involved in public questions, and that they encourage experimentation and innovation in public policy (Dilger 1989; Williamson 1990).

The Argument for Privatization

In recent years a new dimension has been added to the debate over the "who should decide" question. Advocates of privatization have gone beyond the public versus private and centralization versus decentralization debates by questioning the assumption that it is in the public's interest to allow government to provide or regulate specific types of activities and services. Although privatization's theoretical underpinnings can be traced back to the laissez-faire economic theories of Adam Smith, most of its major themes were articulated during the 1960s by conservative economist Milton Friedman and by public choice theorists James Buchanan and Gordon Tullock.

Milton Friedman launched an economic attack on the growth of government by reformulating traditional laissez-faire economic perspectives concerning government's coercive nature. Instead of advocating a reduction in the size of government that also suggested a retreat from protecting the poor and leaving the macroeconomic health of the nation to the vagaries of the business cycle, he advocated a reduction in the size of government as a means to enhance the economic status of the poor and reinvigorate the national economy. He did this by explaining government activity through the analogy of markets. He characterized government as a public monopoly, subject to the same tendencies toward inefficiency, unresponsiveness, and waste that private firms experience in noncompetitive market situations. He also characterized the growth of government regulatory efforts as anti-consumer, arguing that the belief that government regulation protected the public's health, safety, and welfare from the abuses of big businesses solely intent on maximizing profits was a myth. Instead, he argued that much of the government's regulation represented the victory of large businesses or professional interests in the political arena, where they used their political clout to convince legislators to impose licensing and regulatory burdens on new and small businesses as a means to reduce competition in the marketplace.

Friedman also established a distinction between governmental responsibility and government service provision. He acknowledged that the market is unable to adequately supply collective goods because it is relatively easy for consumers to make full use of such goods and services without paying for them (i.e., to be "free riders"). Since suppliers are not certain that they will be paid for providing these goods and services, no one is willing to risk their capital to supply them. Therefore, government must intervene in the market to force collective contributions, usually in the form of taxes or user fees, to assure an adequate supply of the good or service (Friedman 1962; Savas 1987; Henig 1990). However, Friedman also argued that while government may have a role in assuring the adequate supply of goods and services subject to the free-rider problem, it should not be assumed that government should provide the good or service. Instead, government should contract with private firms to supply these goods and services or it should offer vouchers to individual citizens to purchase these goods and services in the private marketplace because, unlike government, contracting out and the provision of vouchers operate in competitive environments that foster efficiency and effectiveness (Henig 1990). Thus, by reducing the size of government and the scope of its activities, Friedman argued that taxpayers would benefit from lower levels of taxation, the poor and the disadvantaged would gain from more effective and efficient government services, and the national economy would be reinvigorated because competition would be restored and fostered in the private sector.

Buchanan and Tullock built on Friedman's work by using his argument that the behavior of public officials and governmental agencies could be explained in the same way that the behavior of consumers and private firms could be explained, through the examination of the rational pursuit of individual self-interest. Using traditional microeconomic analysis, they argued that much of the impetus toward the enlargement of the public sector had little to do with fostering the public good. Instead, rational, self-interested politicians and bureaucrats recognized that by increasing the size and scope of government they also maximized their personal status, power, and financial return. Moreover, because the costs of enlarging the government are spread over a large, usually immobilized constituency, there is relatively little political opposition to its expansion. In contrast, the benefits of an expanded public sector are usually concentrated on limited segments of the population that rally to defend the programs that they have a stake in protecting. The political resilience of the social security program is one such example. As a result, government has an inherent tendency to grow, is inefficient and inequitable, and primarily benefits politicians, bureaucrats, and special interest groups at the expense of taxpayers (Bennett and Dilorenzo 1987; Henig 1990).

Load Shedding, Contracting Out, and Vouchers

To promote efficiency and effectiveness, privatization advocates have argued that government should use the following implementation devices: load shedding, contracting out, and vouchers. Load shedding involves the complete withdrawal of the public sector from providing services that are not subject to the free rider problem. Privatization advocates have argued that many governmental activities fall into this category and that private entrepreneurs would be eager to step in to provide these shedded services and, facing competition from other private sources, would deliver the services in a more efficient and cost-effective manner than government. Even if private entrepreneurs did not step in, then local community organizations and self-help efforts would take up the slack.

When it is determined that a governmental role is appropriate (e.g., for collective goods and programs, such as fire protection in urban areas), then contracting out and vouchers are recommended. Contracting out involves the hiring of private firms to provide services normally handled by public-sector employees. Under this arrangement, public officials determine what needs to be done and solicit bids from private firms that are willing to perform the specified tasks. The competition to obtain these bids forces firms to seek the most cost-efficient procedures and to devise innovative methods for improving the quality of services provided. The government's role is limited to monitoring private sector contractors and regulating corrupt or unfair market practices to ensure the continuation of competitive markets (Henig 1990). Vouchers are grants that can be used by recipients to purchase specified goods or services. By using vouchers, the need for large government bureaucracies is reduced significantly. The most famous voucher system is the food stamp program. Instead of operating government owned and managed farms to produce food for the poor or having government-owned and managed grocery stores for the poor, eligible recipients receive food stamps redeemable for groceries that are grown on privately owned farms and sold in privately owned grocery stores. Privatization advocates argue that vouchers should also be used in education and housing to increase recipient choice concerning where they or their children attend school and where they live (Friedman and Friedman 1979; Henig 1985).

Although the writings of Friedman, Tullock, and Buchanan were widely discussed among academics, they had relatively little immediate impact on national policy. Legitimation of the privatization theory required evidence that market forces could produce public goods and provide public services more efficiently and effectively than government. That evidence came from studies of cities that had contracted with private firms to provide such traditional local government services as fire protection and trash collection.

Privatization in Practice: Cities and Contracting Out

Cities have a long tradition of contracting with private firms to provide public services. For example, San Francisco has contracted out its trash collection services since 1932 (Henig 1990). However, until the 1970s privatization of local government services was the exception not the rule. It was during the 1970s that cities increasingly turned to contracting out as a practical means to reduce the cost of municipal services. At that time, many cities found themselves in great fiscal stress. The national inflation rate had grown to double digits, increasing the cost of providing services significantly. At the same time, local government revenues were restrained by a leveling off, and in some instances an absolute decline, in financial assistance provided by the national government through its grants-in-aid programs. Moreover, the nation experienced a taxpayers' revolt, symbolized by California's Proposition 13 that significantly reduced property tax rates there, which, in most cases, prevented local governments from increasing their revenue by increasing local taxes. In addition, the national economy weakened. As economic activity slowed, so did local tax revenue. As a result, local government expenses continued to go up but their revenue stagnated or declined, creating fiscal stress.

Privatization at the local government level arose as a practical, managerial response to this fiscal stress, not as the result of an ideological movement among the American people or their elected officials (Henig 1990).

Today, private firms are now contracting with thousands of cities to provide virtually every type of local government service (Fixler and Poole 1987). According to one estimate, municipal governments contracted out a total of $22 billion in 1972, $65 billion in 1982, and over $100 billion in 1987. The municipal service most frequently contracted out was solid waste collection and storage, followed by vehicle towing and storage, maintenance of buildings and grounds, and various administrative services such as data processing and debt collection (Nelson 1989).

The first, in-depth studies of an individual city's experiences with contracting out its public services were published in the early 1970s. In 1973, Roger Ahlbrant concluded that Scottsdale, Arizona, and its suburbs were able to provide fire protection to their residents at approximately half the per capita cost of cities of comparable size by contracting out its fire protection services to the Rural/Metro Fire Protection Company (Bendick 1984; Henig 1990). In 1974, E. S. Savas concluded that it cost New York City more than twice as much as the private sector to collect a ton of garbage (Henig 1990). Numerous other studies since then have confirmed that private firms are almost always more cost efficient than government in providing a wide variety of services, from airport administration to zoo maintenance. Contracting out has proven to be particularly successful when it involves services that the private sector already performs on its own, such as trash collection, servicing vehicles, and cleaning offices (Katz 1991). Moreover, many studies have indicated that private firms are able to offer these services at a level of quality that is equivalent to, and in some cases superior to, the level of quality provided by government employees (Bennett and Dilorenzo 1987; Fixler and Poole 1987; Moore 1987; Savas 1987). Finally, local governments have learned valuable lessons from the relatively few instances where contracting out has not led to cost savings or resulted in a reduction in service quality. They now recognize that it is their responsibility to make certain that the contractor adheres to the contract, delivers the service, and handles customer complaints in an efficient and efficacious manner (Katz 1991).

Other Arguments for Privatization

Most of privatization's advocates stress what has been referred to by some as the pragmatic argument. That is, that privatization will improve governmental productivity and, as a result, give taxpayers more service for their money. These advocates focus on cities' experiences with contracting out as proof that privatization should take place.

There are three other arguments that are also presented by privatization's advocates. The first is an ideological argument. Instead of stressing the economic efficiencies promised by a greater reliance on the private sector, it focuses on privatization's role in preserving personal and economic freedom. Individuals who use the ideological argument for privatization fear the intrusive nature of government and the potential misuse of government powers by majorities intent on furthering their own economic and social goals at the expense of the rights of those in the minority (Savas 1987).

Privatization is also sometimes advocated by commercial interests who see substantial business opportunities if privatization were to come about. Finally, some advocate privatization on populist grounds. Populists fear the intrusion of both big government and big business in private lives. They argue that people should have a greater choice in determining the scope and nature of public services than they have now and that they should be empowered to define their common needs and address them without undue reliance on distant, uncaring government bureaucracies. They advocate privatization because they believe it can revive the traditional American ideals of self-discipline and self-help (Henig 1985; Savas 1987; Nelson 1989).

The Argument against Privatization

Those who oppose the privatization movement recognize that there may be short-term, microeconomic benefits to contracting out, load shedding, and the use of vouchers. However, they question the long-term macroeconomic impacts of privatization. They note that the case for privatization as a means of bringing about deep reductions in government activity neglects the contribution of increased public expenditures as a means of assuring stability to the national economy and its financial systems (Starr 1987). Moreover, they also argue that privatization benefits some groups at the expense of others. Many government regulations and services that the advocates of privatization criticize evolved as a direct response to the needs and demands of previously disadvantaged groups, particularly the poor and minorities, that were ignored by the private sector. They contend that privatization would isolate the least advantaged members of American society because private firms have strong economic incentives to skim off the best clients and offer only the most profitable services (Henig 1985; Starr 1987). One example of this skimming off or "creaming" of clients is the Job Training Partnership Act (JTPA). Under pressure to achieve high job-placement rates at a low cost, public administrators in the JTPA program during the late 1980s routinely sought out applicants who required only brief training and screened out those who required substantial educational and job training assistance (Dilger 1989). Privatization's critics argue that creaming of applicants would be universalized if privatization took place, leaving those most in need of public assistance without any help at all (Starr 1987).

Privatization's critics also note that privatization's advocates often fail to point out that much of the cost savings achieved by using private firms comes from their use of lower wage levels for their full time employees and greater use of part-time workers with fewer fringe benefits. Thus, privatization may save taxpayer dollars in the short term, but taxpayers will end up paying more in the long term when these employees become ill and do not have adequate health care insurance or need financial assistance when they retire because they do not have an adequate pension plan. As a result, they do not view privatization as a means to provide public goods and services in a cost-effective and efficient manner. Instead, they regard privatization as an effective means to break unions and diminish the economic status of public employees (Starr 1987).

RCAs and Privatization

Although the privatization literature fails to devote much attention to the role of RCAs in providing public services, the creation of RCA-governed communities is the nation's leading example of load shedding. As illustrated in Table 2.2, RCAs are now offering many services that would otherwise be provided by their local government, including but not limited to trash collection, street repair and lighting, water and sewer services, recreational facilities, and snow removal. As such, RCAs serve as an excellent laboratory for testing the impacts of load shedding at the local government level.

5

RCAs and the Privatization Movement

The growing dissatisfaction with the public sector's performance as a service provider during the 1970s and 1980s may have generated a political environment conducive to the formation of institutions, such as RCAs, that decentralize decisionmaking authority in American society. However, most local government officials continue to view the formation of RCAs as well as the contracting out of various public services to private companies as pragmatic responses to local fiscal stress. Their actions do not reflect their acceptance, or the acceptance on the part of their staff or constituencies, of either the ideological, commercial, or populist arguments presented by privatization's advocates (see Chapter 4). When discussing the pros and cons of various developers' proposals to create PUDs and condominium developments, local government officials typically do not consider the long-term theoretical impacts that RCAs might have on the nature of local public service delivery systems. Instead, they usually discuss with the developer the project's marketability, impact on local traffic patterns and school enrollments, and who will be responsible for the project's infrastructure costs. As a result, load shedding at the local government level has come about almost by default. There has not been a conscious, systematic effort to purposively alter the nature of local public service delivery systems according to the tenets of privatization theory. Nevertheless, the cumulative impact of creating over 150,000 RCAs to date has changed the nature of local public service delivery systems in many communities across the United States. Moreover, as the number of RCAs continues to increase, their cumulative impact on the nature of local public delivery systems is certain to grow.

RCAs' Advocates: The Case for Load Shedding

Most RCAs' CC&Rs empower the board of directors to provide specific services to its members. Most CC&Rs also include specific guidelines and procedures that the board of directors and the general membership must abide by when determining the type and extent of services that the RCA will provide. However, most CC&Rs do not furnish specific guidelines concerning how the board of directors contracts for these services. For example, most CC&Rs do not require the board of directors to seek competitive bids for contracts or to award the contracts to the lowest bidder if there is more than one bid. In addition, most CC&Rs do not prohibit the contracting out of services to firms owned by members of the board of directors or by members of their families. However, as mentioned in Chapter 2, state courts have invalidated RCA actions and have held board members and RCA managers individually liable if they take actions that violate the business judgment rule or if they fail to maintain their fiduciary responsibility to the RCA (Rosenberry 1985, 1989). As a result, RCA board members subject themselves to potential litigation if they fail to contract out their RCA's services in a diligent, reasonable, and prudent manner. Specifically, they may be held liable for all damages to the association, including compensatory damages and court costs and attorney's fees. They are also subject to punitive damages. Moreover, some states impose criminal sanctions if a breach of fiduciary duty is found (Diaz 1988). And, of course, RCA board members are held accountable for their actions on election day when the homeowners can remove them from office.

Although corporate law acts as a deterrent for abusing the award of contracts, most RCA board members are volunteers with little previous experience in running a corporation or dealing with contractors. Some RCA critics have suggested that while some of the larger RCAs can afford to hire professional agencies or individuals to help them contract out their services in a cost-effective manner, they doubt that most RCAs have the expertise to live up to the privatization's advocates promises that load shedding local government services will lead to more effective service provision (better quality) at a lower cost (greater efficiency). However, RCA advocates point out that preliminary studies have indicated that RCAs have provided many public services at a cost of 30 to 60 percent less than local government because they routinely contract out their services to the lowest bidder (Frazier 1984; Garreau 1987). Moreover, several surveys of RCA members have indicated that they are generally satisfied with the services provided by their RCA (Urban Land Institute 1964; Norcross 1973; Dowden 1980; Dilger 1990). For example, 32 percent of the respondents to a recent nationwide survey of RCA board members indicated that their association's membership would rate the association's performance as a service provider as excellent and 63 percent thought that their members would rate their association's performance as good. Only 4 percent of the respondents thought that their membership would rate their association's performance as a service provider as being fair and less than one percent thought that they would rate their association as a poor service provider (Dilger 1990).

It can be argued that RCA board members are likely to overestimate their memberships' satisfaction with their association's performance as a service provider because they are, as board members, at least indirectly responsible for service delivery. However, earlier surveys of both RCA board members and rank-and-file members also concluded that there was a very high level of satisfaction with the association's performance as a service provider. For example, one of the earliest nationwide surveys of RCA members was conducted by the Urban Land Institute in 1962. They asked RCA members from 233 RCAs located throughout the United States if they were satisfied, neutral, or dissatisfied with their RCA's performance in maintaining the development's common areas and in supplying services. Eighty-one percent of the respondents indicated that they were satisfied with their RCA's performance as a service provider, 11 percent indicated that they were neutral on this question, and only 8 percent indicated that they were dissatisfied with their RCA's performance (Urban Land Institute 1964). A 1973 survey of RCAs located on the east and west coasts did not specifically ask respondents to rate their RCA's performance as a service provider. However, it did ask them to indicate how they would rate the quality of their RCA's living conditions. Although this question does not measure in a precise way how RCA members view their RCA's performance as a service provider, since the quality of the RCA's living conditions is directly affected by the RCA's performance as a service provider the response does reflect, at least to some extent, members' views on this issue. In that study, 86 percent of the respondents rated the quality of life in their RCA as being either good or excellent. A similar study conducted in 1976 by the Washington Metropolitan Council of Governments in the Washington, D. C., area found that 79 percent of the respondents there rated their overall living conditions as being either good or excellent (Dowden 1980). Subsequent surveys of RCA members conducted during the 1980s, and now, during the 1990s, have indicated that the majority of RCA members have continued to express their overall satisfaction with the living conditions within their RCA and with their association's performance as a service provider. Moreover, the percentage of respondents indicating that they are satisfied with their RCA's performance as a service provider has been rising. Eighty-one percent of RCA members indicated that were satisfied with their RCA's performance as a service provider in 1962. In 1990, 95 percent of RCA board members indicated that they believed that their members would rate their association as either an excellent or good service provider.

The 1990 survey also asked RCA board members if there were any services currently offered by their RCA that could be provided more efficiently by their local government. An overwhelming majority of the respondents (78%) said no. Of those who did believe that local government could provide one or more of their services more efficiently than their community association, the most frequently named services were street lighting and street repair (Dilger 1990).

Besides touting RCAs' performance as effective and efficient service providers, RCA's advocates also note that because RCA's jurisdictional boundaries are generally smaller than the typical local government they are better able to meet the public's varying preferences for public goods and services, such as the frequency of trash collection or the provision and extent of recreational facilities. Since both the preferences and the ability to pay for public goods and services vary from household to household, the smaller the governing entity's jurisdiction, the more likely it is that the governing entity can respond in a precise manner to these varying preferences and abilities to pay. In contrast, the larger a governing entity becomes the more likely it will produce a uniform level of goods and services that will be viewed as being profligate and exceedingly expensive in some neighborhoods and inadequate and parsimonious in others.

Recognizing that preferences for specific types of housing and commonly provided services varies according to each family's individual circumstances, developers of relatively large condominium and planned unit developments have recently begun to subdivide their projects into specific subcategories in an effort to enhance their project's marketability. For example, it is not uncommon for a large condominium or planned unit development to have one section consisting of housing designed to meet the needs of the elderly, another designed for the first-time home buyer, and another for the move-up home buyer. Recognizing that the buyers interested each of these subcategories of housing tend to have significant differences in their ability to pay for public goods and services and that their preferences for particular types of public goods and services, such as the provision of tot lots and playground equipment, also differ, most developers now create an RCA for each section of their development instead of having a single RCA for the entire neighborhood. In this way, home buyers in each section of the development are better able to obtain the type and extent of services appropriate for that section (Peterson 1990).

RCAs' advocates also point to poignant success stories to buttress their claims that RCAs can and should be allowed to provide services normally associated with local government. Although most

RCAs are created as part of a new housing development, they have also been created within existing neighborhoods. The Waterman Place Association in St. Louis is one example. It was established in 1974 when more than 90 percent of the property owners in the neighborhood agreed to form the association. Plagued by crime and prostitution, the neighborhood's property values had plummeted. The association successfully petitioned the city government to transfer title to the main street serving their neighborhood. The association agreed to maintain the street at its own expense and borrowed the necessary funds to erect a gate to limit traffic through the area. It also used its covenant-backed power to levy assessments as collateral to secure financing for neighborhood improvements. Within a year, property values in the neighborhood doubled and by the mid-1980s were five times higher than they were the year prior to the formation of the homeowners' association. In the Bronx, New York, a large privately owned apartment complex housing 12,000 people underwent a similar transformation. Plagued by rampant crime and physical deterioration, the Glen Oaks Village apartment development converted to a cooperative in 1980. Using assessments to finance a neighborhood security patrol, crime was reduced significantly. Moreover, assessments were used to repair and maintain neighborhood streets, sidewalks, and playing areas and to collect the neighborhood's trash. As the neighborhood's graffiti and trash were brought under control and its streets and sidewalks spruced up, the neighborhood's property values began to rise, as did the neighborhood's pride. RCAs have produced similar effects on decaying neighborhoods in Baltimore, Tulsa, and Kansas City (Frazier 1984).

In St. Louis County, there are over 400 private street associations. These RCAs are responsible for various services involving their subdivision's streets, including, but not limited to street maintenance, repair, sweeping, and snow removal. A recent study of fifty-three of these associations revealed that the overall condition of the RCAs' streets was as good or better than most other streets in St. Louis County. The study also concluded that the RCAs were better able than local government to accommodate diversity in preferences for street-related services among neighborhoods. These preferences varied significantly among the subdivisions studied. Some subdivisions wanted additional street lighting and were willing to assess themselves to get it while others did not. Some wanted a large array of street-related services and were willing to assess themselves to obtain them while other subdivisions wanted only the basic services of street repair and snow removal. Thus, the study concluded that the St. Louis County experience with RCAs suggest that they are feasible units of service provision for local public goods and services when those goods and services generate benefits that flow primarily to the immediate neighborhood. The study noted that residential street repair, snow removal, tree trimming, and street lighting were local public services ideally suited for RCAs (Oakerson 1989a).

A Different Argument for RCAs

Most of those who view the formation of RCAs favorably focus on what can be called the pragmatic argument. That is, they focus on their ability to provide certain services more efficiently and effectively than local government and on their ability to better accommodate the diversity of preferences for service levels among neighborhoods. They also note that RCAs have a favorable impact on property values. However, some of RCAs' advocates would support the formation of RCAs even if they were not better service providers than local government and they did not enhance property values. Taking a populist approach, they are more concerned with the issues of control and representation than they are with service provision. In their view, the relatively recent expansion of the public sector has seriously diminished the decisionmaking authority of society's value building and supportive institutions, such as the church and family. The demise of these institutions has, in turn, fostered a political environment that is not only marked by increased governmental control over nearly every aspect of private life but by widespread apathy, ignorance, and a sense of helplessness among the general public toward governmental institutions. Lacking political knowledge, effective lobbying skills, and social mechanisms that promote collective action, the typical citizen recognizes that he or she does not have the resources to compete in the political process with well-financed and politically sophisticated lobby organizations. As a result, the number of people believing in the old adage that "you can't fight city hall," who believe that the political system is biased toward the wealthy and special interests, and who opt out of the political system altogether continues to increase. Moreover, the public's disillusionment with the political process and its institutions constitutes a growing threat to the legitimacy of the public sector's decisions. It is difficult, if not impossible, for the public sector to reach decisions that are representative of the public's interest if the public is not participating in the political process.

RCA advocates are convinced that RCAs should be applauded because they provide ordinary citizens an opportunity to play a significant role in determining their neighborhood's future. Instead of relying on government bureaucrats and policymakers to make important decisions on behalf of the neighborhood, RCAs encourage neighbors to assume the initiative and to take an active part in determining their neighborhood's future themselves. As a result, RCAs serve to restrict the scope of the government's control over private lives. Moreover, by encouraging their members to engage in the process of self-governance, RCAs also encourage their members to become more knowledgeable about the activities of their local government and how its decisions affect their neighborhood's property values and quality of life. Thus, by encouraging ordinary people to become more aware of the political world and how its decisions affect their lives and by offering them a mechanism to participate in their local government's political processes, RCAs foster a more just and legitimate society. They do this by encouraging members to use their heightened knowledge of local political processes and outcomes to hold local policymakers more accountable to their interests as opposed to the interests of organized interest groups.

RCAs' Critics: The Case against Load Shedding

RCAs' critics argue while it may be true that some RCAs are able to provide some services in a more efficient manner than their local government, these cost savings are available to only those RCAs that have economies of scale large enough and a management capacity sophisticated enough to deal effectively with contractors. The typical RCA, with only thirty to forty units, does not have an economy of scale large enough to bargain effectively with most contractors. Moreover, unlike the larger associations, they do not have an off-site management company negotiating on their behalf. Instead, they rely on the management and leadership abilities of those who are elected to their board of directors. In many instances, particularly with smaller RCAs, the management abilities of their board of directors are questionable. Often, these individuals are volunteers with little or no previous experience in negotiating contracts or securing services. For example, a survey of Florida condominium residents revealed that 62 percent of them either strongly agreed or agreed that most condominium officers lacked the technical training to be effective managers (Williamson and Adams 1987). Moreover, a California study revealed that many of the smaller RCAs there had a very difficult time finding people willing to serve on their board and an even more difficult time finding board members willing to give the time necessary to manage the association's affairs. The study indicated that 19 percent of the RCAs in California relied on a single board member to do all the work for the association and 3 percent had no one on their board who had the time to conduct the association's business. The study also revealed that the typical board of directors' member serves for only two years. This high turnover rate further diminishes the board's capacity to manage the affairs of the association in an efficacious manner (Barton and Silverman 1987a). Thus, the California and Florida studies suggest that many RCA board of directors are ill equipped to bargain effectively with contractors.

RCAs' critics also dispute the notion that RCAs are better able than local government to meet the diversity of preferences among various neighborhoods for services and related fees. Although it may appear that by transferring governmental functions to RCAs consumers are given a greater choice of options because they can choose to purchase a home in a subdivision serviced by the local government or in a subdivision serviced by an RCA that more closely matches their desire for amenities and fees, this is not the case. In many housing markets, particularly in California and Florida, consumers' choice is relatively limited because most of the available housing is organized as RCAs, and most RCAs offer similar services and fees. Moreover, many consumers are not sufficiently knowledgeable about the housing alternatives available to them to make an informed choice. Part of the blame for this lack of information can be placed on sales personnel in RCA-governed neighborhoods who are ill informed and reticent about conveying the precise nature of ownership in RCA-governed communities to potential home buyers. Part of the blame can also be placed on RCA-governing documents and other association records that are of little use to potential home buyers because they are written in legal jargon that defies the ability of the typical home buyer to comprehend them. And part of the blame can be placed on home buyers who generally equate the purchase of a home with the sole right to determine its use. As a result, most home buyers do not press sales personnel for additional information or demand that RCA-governing documents be fully explained to them prior to purchasing their home. One study has suggested that as many as 85 percent of home buyers are not fully aware of the neighborhood's CC&Rs and the role of their RCA in enforcing those CC&Rs when they purchase their home in an RCA-governed community (Winokur 1989a). Moreover, even if the home buyer is fully informed and has other housing alternatives available, there is no guarantee that the association they buy into will maintain its particular offering of services and assessment fees. RCAs' memberships are in constant flux as property changes hands and renters move in and out of the neighborhood. Since the level of services and assessments offered in RCAs are determined by vote, members may find that as the neighborhood changes the level of services or assessments offered no longer meet their desires. Although homeowners unhappy with their RCA have the option to move, this has high personal and financial costs. As one study concluded, to the extent that home buyers have a choice about moving into a RCA-governed community, that choice is typically poorly informed and there are very high costs involved in making a new choice. As such, the mandatory RCA is as much an involuntary association as any small town government (Barton and Silverman 1989).

To prove the inadequacy of the consumer choice argument,

RCAs' critics point to the actual behavior of residents and homeowners in RCA-governed neighborhoods. The vast majority (93%) of RCAs in a California study conducted in 1986 reported problems with violations of the association's rules and one-quarter of RCAs there reported at least one violation so intractable that they were unable to resolve the problem. The most frequent problem cited by the respondents involved residents making unauthorized changes in their dwelling units. In addition, 44 percent of the RCA board members there reported that they were personally harassed, openly accused, or threatened with a lawsuit by a member of their association during the previous twelve-month period. Moreover, nationally, the amount of litigation actually filed by RCA members challenging their RCA's enforcement of the neighborhood's CC&Rs increased steadily from 1957 to 1977, grew by more than seven-fold between 1977 and 1982 and doubled again from 1982 to 1987 (Winokur 1989a). The California survey revealed that 5 percent of all associations there reported that they had been sued by one of their members during the previous year (Barton and Silverman 1987a).

RCAs' critics argue that such extensive rule violations, expressions of anger, and filing of lawsuits indicate that most RCAs contain people who do not desire the particular mix of services, regulations, and assessments offered by their association. While some people may have the financial resources and knowledge to select a RCA-governed community that matches their individual desires for services, regulations, and assessments, most residents and homeowners in RCA-governed communities find themselves in situations that violate their expectations (Barton and Silverman 1987a).

RCAs' critics also argue that even if all RCAs were more efficient and effective than local governments in providing services and they did accommodate the preferences of their membership concerning services, regulations, and assessments, they would still object to their use because RCAs operate on the principle of fiscal equivalence—where members get what they pay for and pay for what they get. This can present problems for RCA members who are on fixed incomes or who suffer a loss of income. When illness, unemployment, retirement, or other event reduces the income of a homeowner who does not reside in a RCA-governed neighborhood, he or she can defer maintenance expenses or use their own labor to reduce maintenance expenses. This flexibility is lost in RCA-governed communities because RCAs are required to protect the neighborhood's property values by maintaining a uniform standard. If an individual member can no longer afford to pay the assessment, even if he or she voted against the provision of specific services, the association will attempt to collect payment and, as a last resort, can place a lien on the member's home (Barton and Silverman 1988; ACIR 1989).

Recognizing that the principle of fiscal equivalence can present a problem for some association members, several larger RCAs offer some of their more expensive services, such as membership in the community clubhouse, on an optional, cafeteria-style basis. In this way, members have more flexibility in determining their service levels and can adjust their assessment fees in accordance with their desire for services and/or ability to pay. However, most RCAs do not have economies of scale that enable them to allow their members to opt out of services approved by the majority of its members (Kleine 1989).

A Different Argument against RCAs

Although most of RCAs' critics emphasize their shortcomings in providing services in an efficient and effective manner and in meeting their members' expectations, some also object to them on ideological grounds. Like the Progressives of the early 1900s, these critics are suspicious of the private sector and reject the notion that localism and diversity are to be promoted. Instead, they view government as an appropriate mechanism to tone down the economic inequities created by the private marketplace and the social inequities, particularly regarding racism, that often accompany localism and the promotion of diversity. For example, these critics value government's ability to redistribute income and other resources among income groups and are bothered by RCA's principle of fiscal equivalence. They also value government's role in fostering a commitment to shared goals that bind the nation together as one people. They view RCAs as mechanisms to segregate the population according to income, social status, social values, and other personal characteristics that define neighborhoods composed primarily of homeowners as opposed to renters. Although this segregation is an asset when seen in the context of enhancing the neighborhood's identity and sense of community, it is a detriment when viewed in the context of a broader sense of metropolitan, state, or national community (Nelson 1989).

Ironically, RCAs are also criticized by some as a threat to personal identity and individual freedom and autonomy. These critics view a person's home as one of the last bastions of personal liberty and privacy. In their view, the home bears a special relationship to the owner's personal identity and homeowners should be allowed to express their own distinctive personalities by controlling the details of their homes' uses. Although they admit that the enforcement of CC&Rs have created some residential developments of striking beauty, they are convinced that RCAs are contributing to what they refer to as the commodification of the American landscape, where every suburb and downtown area increasingly resembles all others. This commodification, in turn, has created a crisis of personal identity in America, where it is increasingly difficult for anyone to shape their own life according to their own unique values. Traditionally, home ownership has played a central role in enriching the sense of individual identity in the United States. However, RCAs' CC&Rs are increasingly limiting the ability of individuals to express their unique personalities in their residences. In their view, many of the restrictions found in RCAs' CC&Rs, especially those addressing neighborhood aesthetics, are inappropriate. They believe that respect for personal identity requires protection of each resident's right to determine when they can take out the trash, to select the color of the family swing set, to fly the American (or other) flag from their balcony, to choose their own interior curtains and liners and to decide how many sixteenths of an inch thick the plexiglass shall be on their balcony enclosure (Winokur 1989b).

These critics also question the assumption of RCA's advocates that home buyers in RCA-governed communities freely and knowingly consent to the restrictions in their CC&Rs in exchange for the promise of higher property values and more uniform community aesthetics. Moreover, they worry that many of the restrictions in CC&Rs are not only inappropriate infringements on personal liberty but if applied by governmental bodies would be found to be unconstitutional. For example, although national legislation now prohibits discrimination in housing against families with children, until recently many RCAs prohibited residents from having children and others prohibited residents from being married. Some RCAs even regulate religious practices and others have restricted commercial and political speech within the boundaries of the development (Winokur 1989b).

RCAs and Load Shedding: Some Practical Concerns

Although academics and others are very interested in the impacts that RCAs are having on service delivery systems and personal liberties, local officials are often less concerned with these issues than they are with several immediate and practical issues raised by the creation of RCAs. One of these issues is the extent of the responsibility, if any, that local governments have in the event a RCA in their jurisdiction goes bankrupt or is otherwise unable to provide services to its members. Although relatively few RCAs have ever gone bankrupt, many have approached local governments asking for fiscal assistance following an unforeseen financial setback (Longhini and Mosena 1978; Dowden 1980). Moreover, many of the nation's older RCAs, formed during the 1950s and 1960s, are increasingly facing major renovation projects as their streets and sewer systems deteriorate with age. Lacking sufficient reserves to meet these large costs, many of these RCAs have imposed very large assessments on their members and are increasingly looking to their local governments for financial assistance (Peterson 1990).

Local governments are not required by any law or statute to provide services to a neighborhood whose association runs into financial difficulty. However, most local governments have enacted ordinances that allow them to step in and provide services if a financial difficulty should arise. In the absence of a specific ordinance dealing with RCAs, many local governments have generic ordinances that allow them to perform maintenance functions on private property if the public health, safety, or welfare is threatened. In both instances, local governments generally do not use public funds to provide these services. Instead, they assess the individual unit owners the cost of providing the services (Dowden 1980).

Ironically, although local governments provide mechanisms to take over common areas and infrastructure costs from financially troubled RCAs, the typical local government does not regulate RCA finances in any way (Dowden 1980). States generally do not regulate RCA finances either. California is one of the few exceptions. It requires RCAs to conduct a reserve study that reviews the physical components of all commonly owned property and produce a financial plan for their eventual replacement. The reserve study requirement keeps owners informed of their ongoing liability for future renovations and, since the reserve study must be disclosed to anyone considering the purchase of a home in the RCA, it also ensures that resell buyers are also aware of their liability. In addition, since 1988 California has prohibited RCAs there from increasing their regular assessment fees by more than 20 percent or emergency assessment fees by more than 5 percent unless the increases are approved by a majority vote of its members, with the stipulation that at least half of the membership voted (Peterson 1990).

Since local governments are potentially affected by RCA financial activities, those who view RCAs critically argue that the first thing state and local governments should do is to require all RCAs within their jurisdictions to incorporate. Most of the smaller RCAs in the United States are not incorporated and are self-managed. As a result, government officials have very little knowledge of their activities or financial status and, if they want to offer them information or advice, have a difficult time finding them. Incorporation would provide government a list of all RCAs within their jurisdiction. It would also give government an opportunity to build an ongoing and constructive relationship with RCAs instead of hearing from them only after a problem or crisis has occurred. Once RCAs are incorporated, government should then require all of them to periodically conduct a reserve study similar to the one required by California. The reserve study should be made available to all of the RCA's members, anyone interested in buying a home in the RCA, and to its local government officials. RCAs should also be required to meet certain financial tests, such as placing an amount equal to 75 percent of its annual budget in a reserve account to cover any unanticipated expenses (Barton and Silverman 1987a).

Another practical issue that arises out of the privatization of public services to RCAs concerns tax equity. Several tax equity issues were discussed in Chapter 2. The most important of these issues for most RCA members is that they are assessed local property taxes at the same rate as other property owners in their town or city. They are also assessed a special fee by their RCA to pay for their neighborhood's infrastructure costs and other services. Although a portion of these fees are used for services that directly benefit only the members of the association and are not normally provided by government, such as exterior maintenance of buildings and exclusive use of a swimming pool or clubhouse, a portion of these fees are used to pay for services that local government provides to other members of the community without any additional fee beyond their property tax collections. Thus, RCA members are often taxed for services, such as snow or trash removal, that they have already paid for and provided themselves. RCA members argue that this is unfair and point out that it also makes it more difficult for RCAs to perform their function as a source of affordable housing. To promote tax equity and enhance the supply of affordable housing, they want local governments to follow the example set by Houston, Texas, Kansas City, Missouri, and Montgomery County, Maryland, which provide RCA members a property tax rebate commensurate with the cost savings realized from the RCA's provision of services.

Most local governments have refused to provide RCA members a tax rebate. Because increased intergovernmental funding is not an option for most local governments, a tax rebate for RCA members would require them to either raise local taxes or reduce services in other areas of their community. Neither of these options are politically attractive. However, as the number of RCA members nationwide continue to increase, tax rebates are certain to become an important political issue in many local campaigns.

Moreover, as demonstrated in the next chapter, tax equity issues are rapidly challenging zoning and development issues as the leading topic for discussion between RCA board members and local government officials.

Ironically, RCAs, which are criticized for failing to redistribute service costs among their members, provide local governments property tax revenue that is routinely redistributed to other neighborhoods. This fact is often overlooked by RCA critics who maintain that local governments abdicate their responsibility to provide affordable housing when they approve PUD and condominium developments. Instead of emphasizing the formation of RCAs which often have assessment fees that are prohibitively expensive for those with modest incomes, they argue that local governments should use their zoning authority to allow developers to build houses on smaller lot sizes, to reduce development costs and housing prices, and then place public parks and other recreational amenities within walking distance of these homes. In this way, people of modest means can buy a home and have access to desirable amenities without the burden of assessment fees (Barton and Silverman 1989).

Although this alternative strategy for affordable housing seems sound, it assumes that local governments have both sufficient revenue to offer these public amenities as well as the political will to redistribute property tax revenue away from more affluent neighborhoods toward less affluent ones. The irony of the situation is that the formation of RCAs gives local governments revenue that can be used to undertake the affordable housing strategy advocated by RCAs' critics. Of course, in an era of strained local fiscal circumstances, many local governments cannot afford redistribution, even with the relief provided by RCAs.

6

RCAs and Local Government Interaction

A RCA board president recently wrote to the editors of *CAI News*, a publication of the Community Associations Institute, informing them that several members of his board wanted their RCA to become more involved in civic and political matters (CAI News 1989). He wrote that they were particularly concerned about nearby development and potential traffic congestion. He asked the editors to comment on the relationship that other RCAs had with their local government officials. The editors indicated that most RCAs were so busy running their own affairs that they generally did not have enough time to get involved in civic or political matters. However, they noted that some RCAs had established an external affairs committee that served as an informational clearinghouse concerning what was going on with regard to school board meetings, nearby construction plans, local elections, and other local issues of possible interest to the association's members. The editors also noted that these committees typically passed on this information in a neutral fashion, usually as an informational item in the RCA's newsletter. Their purpose was not to persuade the RCA's membership to advocate a particular position but to give them the information necessary to make an intelligent decision. The editors went on to caution the writer that it was risky for RCAs to get involved in local political affairs because some of their members might object to spending the RCA's money on matters outside its major purposes. They cited a case in New York

City where several condominium unit owners successfully sued their condominium association for spending association funds to fight the developer of a nearby parcel of land. The court ruled that the RCA's bylaws were quite strict in what constituted a common expense and that action of the condominium board violated those bylaws. The editors closed their response by indicating that RCA board members should remember that in a voluntary civic association membership is voluntary, dues are nominal, and a member can easily resign if he or she disagrees with the position or actions of the association. In contrast, membership in an RCA is mandatory, dues are a significant household expense, and those who disagree with the positions taken by their RCA can resign only by selling their homes.

The *CAI News'* editors' caution against RCAs engaging in political activities and their view of RCAs as having a relatively passive role in local political affairs contrasts sharply with the image presented in the nation's leading newspapers concerning RCAs' political activities. These articles suggest that RCAs are very active in local political affairs, that they regularly lobby their local government officials and that they have been very effective in changing local government decisions (Vesey 1983; Marchese 1987; Hornblower 1988). This chapter examines the relationship between RCAs and local government officials and attempts to determine the extent of RCAs' political activities and their impact on local government decisions and behavior.

When discussing the interaction of neighborhood organizations with local government officials a fundamental distinction must be drawn between the activities of voluntary neighborhood civic associations and residential community associations. Although they share the objective of fostering a particular neighborhood's interests, there are important organizational differences between the groups that affect the way they operate, the activities they undertake, and their relationship with local government officials.

Voluntary Neighborhood Civic Associations in Urban Areas

Voluntary neighborhood civic associations have a long political history in the United States. They can be found in almost every urban community throughout the country. Typically, they are formed in response to something bad that has happened in the neighborhood, such as the arrival of a street gang or other criminal element that threatens the residents' security or the accumulation of garbage that attracts rats and other vermin that threaten their health. Their goal is to get local government officials to do something to solve the problem. Of course, not every neighborhood in distress forms itself into a neighborhood civic association. Like many other organized interest groups, most civic associations are initially formed and sustained primarily through the efforts of one or a few outspoken activists in the neighborhood who have the time, energy, personality, and organizational skills necessary to galvanize the neighborhood and to articulate its demands (Clark and Wilson 1961; Salisbury 1969).

Until recently, most neighborhood civic associations were very strident in style and confrontational in expression. Believing that their problems were being neglected by local government officials who were primarily interested in appeasing white, middle-class voters and revitalizing downtown shopping centers, neighborhood civic associations in black and poor neighborhoods often resorted to protests and marches to gain media attention and to pressure local officials into doing something to help them directly (Katz 1990). Reflecting this confrontational approach, local government officials were often outspoken in their opposition to attempts by many civic associations to bypass the local political power structure entirely by seeking direct financing from the national government to provide services for their neighborhood's residents and to finance neighborhood development projects. Citing their accountability to the voters for local development efforts and the provision of local services, many mayors and city council members during the 1960s were vehemently opposed to the national government's Office of Economic Opportunity's (OEO) community action programs. These programs mandated maximum feasible participation by the residents of the areas to be served when determining the program's activities. In the elected officials' view, OEO's community action programs were providing radicals and other political activists with the financial resources to maintain their operations and create a platform for spreading their revolutionary ideas.

This, in turn, resulted in increasing tensions between the poor and existing governmental agencies, fostered class struggle, and did little to enhance the quality of life for the poor and minorities in their communities. However, it did much to enhance the political fortunes of extremists (Judd 1988).

Although protest is still one of the weapons available to neighborhood civic associations located in impoverished areas, the tactics of confrontation and conflict are no longer widespread. Mass protest has given away to collaboration as neighborhood civic associations seek partners to provide some of the services and development projects that they believe their neighborhoods need and their local government is either unwilling or, increasingly, unable to provide (Katz 1990).

Neighborhood activists in poorer neighborhoods have moved away from the tactics of confrontation because they recognize that many cities no longer have the financial resources to correct their neighborhood's problems. They know that the national government has reduced its funding for Community Development Block Grants and other programs that cities have traditionally relied upon to finance neighborhood revitalization efforts. They also know that many cities are experiencing severe financial difficulties because their revenues have been constrained by local taxpayers' revolts, symbolized by California's Proposition 13 that reduced property tax rates there, and deteriorating tax bases resulting from the mass exodus of middle-class, taxpaying residents to the suburbs. As a result, neighborhood activists recognize that while their local government can help, they also need to turn to other sources for financial assistance. Increasingly, they are turning to churches, foundations, banks, and corporations to serve as partners in providing services to neighborhood residents and financing neighborhood development efforts.

According to the National Congress for Community Economic Development, neighborhood civic associations have been able to muster the resources necessary to build nearly 125,000 housing units in the United States, mostly for low-income residents. They have also developed 16.4 million square feet of retail space, offices, and other industrial developments. In addition, in many large cities, neighborhood civic associations are now integral parts of the political landscape as municipal governments routinely provide them operating grants and project funding. Moreover, neighborhood civic associations are active in political affairs in many cities. They routinely provide campaign contributions and volunteers to leaflet their neighborhood on behalf of those local government officials who the civic association's leadership considers to have been helpful. They also work to unseat local government officials who oppose their efforts (Katz 1990).

Voluntary Neighborhood Civic Associations in the Suburbs

Since the 1960s, voluntary neighborhood civic associations have spread to the suburbs. The typical neighborhood civic association in the suburbs is formed for the same reason as it is in urban areas: because something bad has happened in the neighborhood or someone is proposing to do something perceived by the residents as being bad for the neighborhood. Like their urban counterparts, not every suburban neighborhood in distress will form itself into a neighborhood civic association. Usually, they are formed and sustained primarily through the efforts of one or a few outspoken activists who live in the neighborhood and have the time, energy, personality, and organizational skills necessary to galvanize the neighborhood into a political force and articulate its demands to government officials. The one significant difference between suburban and urban neighborhood civic associations is the issues that they typically address. Most suburban neighborhood civic associations are less interested than their urban counterparts in the provision of social services and in the acquisition of resources to finance redevelopment projects that are designed to improve the neighborhood's aesthetic appearance. Instead, they are more concerned with preserving their neighborhood's property values and maintaining its current aesthetic appearance. As a result, suburban neighborhood civic associations are in the vanguard of what has been called the NIMBY—Not In My Back Yard—movement. Adopting the tactics of the urban neighborhood civic associations of an earlier generation, some of today's suburban neighborhood civic associations have resorted to protest and marches to attract public attention to their plight in an effort to prevent their local government from taking various actions that they perceive will make it more difficult to sell their homes, depress their property values, or cause a decline in their quality of life. The issues in contention have ranged from proposals to rezone land near or adjacent to their neighborhoods to allow either higher density housing, commercial or industrial uses, to proposals to locate unwanted public facilities near or adjacent to their neighborhoods, such as hazardous waste dump sites, solid waste landfills, prisons, airports, drug and alcohol rehabilitation centers, and group homes for the mentally retarded (Hornblower 1988).

Civic Associations' Limitations

Much of the debate over voluntary neighborhood civic associations has involved their tactics. Many analysts and policymakers object to them because they tend to resort to what has been referred to as the outsiders' lobbying strategies. Perceiving that policymakers are indifferent to their situation and lacking any enduring relationship with them, neighborhood civic associations often resort to protest and marches to focus public attention on their problem. Although these tactics often succeed in gaining the attention of policymakers who are concerned that the public will perceive them as being insensitive to the needs of its residents, it also generates a varying degree of animosity, ranging from irritation to rage, from policymakers who are accustomed to working through established procedures that are designed to defuse conflict.

The right of neighbors to form into a formal, organized interest group and collectively lobby for or against a particular governmental decision, or to seek financial assistance from the government and, more recently, from the private sector has never been questioned. From the media and citizen's perspective, the right to petition the government for redress of grievances is guaranteed by the First Amendment to the Constitution. Moreover, from the social scientist's perspective, civic associations are generally viewed as legitimate actors in the pluralistic political process. Their activities serve to countervail existing power relationships, creating a healthy sense of competition that helps to produce better public policy (Loomis and Cigler 1986).

Now that neighborhood civic associations in impoverished areas have moved toward a more collaborative, working relationship with "the establishment" and recognizing that the marches and protests undertaken by suburban neighborhood civic associations are the exception, not the rule and that their efforts are primarily aimed at changing governmental decisions and not the governmental system itself, most analysts focus their evaluations of neighborhood civic associations on their ability to effect change in their neighborhoods. In most instances, this ultimately boils down to their ability to alter local governmental decisions and to obtain, and then successfully manage, financial resources to improve their neighborhood.

Most analysts approve of neighborhood civic associations' efforts to upgrade their neighborhoods, believe that they have very good intentions, and recognize that they have a documented and impressive record in altering governmental decisions. However, they also note that neighborhood civic associations have a mixed record in managing financial resources provided by the public and private sectors. This is primarily attributed to two factors. First, neighborhood civic association leaders often prove to be poor administrators. Although they usually have charismatic personalities and excellent interpersonal skills—attributes useful to both a good administrator as well as an effective neighborhood organizer/lobbyist—they often have little or no experience with managing neighborhood redevelopment projects or with the provision of social services. Moreover, in most instances, they are volunteers who have other jobs or family responsibilities that take precedence in their lives. As a result, neighborhood civic associations are subject to frequent turnover among their leadership. This, in turn, creates serious implementation problems.

The second factor affecting neighborhood civic association's management performance is that they tend to be short-lived because they are subject to the free rider problem.

The Free Rider Problem

Mancur Olson argued effectively in his 1965 book, *The Logic of Collective Action,* that the pluralist argument concerning the public sector's decisionmaking processes is flawed because it assumes that interest groups emerge more or less automatically when changes in the political environment render them necessary (Schlozman and Tierney 1986). He suggested that the historical record indicates that countervailing interest groups often do not emerge even when circumstances such as poverty or discrimination would seem to require it. Using "the rational man" model employed by economists to study the behavior of firms, Olson argued that countervailing interest groups did not materialize as expected because in many instances individuals calculate that the cost of membership (attending meetings, paying dues, etc.) exceeds the benefits that the interest group can provide because most interest groups provide collective benefits. Collective benefits accrue to all people in a particular situation or category, regardless of their organizational affiliations. For example, if an educational lobby organization persuades government to take actions that result in an increase in teachers' salaries, all teachers benefit, even ones who are not dues paying members of the organization. Olson concluded that under such circumstances a "rational" self-interested individual would choose not to bear the costs of group participation (i.e., for neighborhood civic association members the cost would be the time and effort expended to attend meetings, leaflet the neighborhood, call or write their elected officials, etc.) because they recognize that they can enjoy the benefits of those activities regardless of their level of involvement in the organization. Realizing that their individual efforts will not appreciably enhance the organization's ability to obtain its goals, the rational individual allows others to assume the organizational burdens and waits to reap the collective benefits. In other words, they become free riders. Because everyone has an incentive to become a free rider, the countervailing interest group generally does not materialize (Olson 1965; Schlozman and Tierney 1986).

Olson argued that interest groups would form and survive only if certain specific conditions in the political environment were present to overcome the free rider phenomena. For example, government routinely coerces individuals to participate in the provision of collective goods, such as national defense, by taxing them. However, unlike government, interest groups generally do not have the ability to coerce potential members to either join or participate in its efforts to provide them with collective goods. However, if the interest group's constituency is particularly small, Olson argued that rational individuals may calculate that it is in their interest to bear the costs of participating in the group's effort. They are likely to reach this conclusion if they believe that their individual effort will have a significant impact on the organization's ability to secure the desired benefit. Thus, in a small group, rational individuals may determine that if they became free riders that they will be denied the collective good. However, in most instances, interest groups represent relatively large constituencies where individual efforts are generally not considered significant. In this case, interest groups will form and survive only if they provide individual members with selective benefits. These are benefits that are available only to those affiliated with the group. Since the only way to receive these benefits is to participate in the group's activities, individuals have an incentive not to become free riders. Olson noted that organizations in the best possible position to offer selective benefits are those initially formed for nonpolitical purposes that ordinarily provide material benefits to their members, such as discounts or access to information that is available only to the organization's members (Olson 1965; Loomis and Cigler 1986).

Olson's work is generally regarded as a seminal contribution to the literature on interest groups. Since the publication of his book in 1965 several other scholars have followed his lead in examining interest group formation. They have concluded that group size may not play as important a role in group formation as Olson thought and that the motivation for group formation extend beyond the provision of selective benefits. As James Q. Wilson has argued, people join organizations for a variety of reasons such as the desire for status, power, money, or simply because a friend asked them to join. He classified the incentives to join an interest group into three categories: material, solidary, and purposive.

Material incentives are similar to selective benefits in that they are tangible resources such as discounts or goods and services that one cannot obtain unless a member of the organization. Solidary incentives are intangible benefits that individuals receive from joining a group, such as an enhanced sense of self-esteem and prestige or the emotional gratification that can accompany organizational membership. Finally, purposive incentives concern the individual's commitment to the organization's goals. Some individuals join organizations because they receive a sense of satisfaction that derives from contributing to a worthwhile goal (Wilson 1973; Schlozman and Tierney 1986).

Olson's theory of group formation and survival and Wilson's modification of that theory help to explain why many neighborhoods in distress do not form voluntary neighborhood civic associations. On the one hand, neighborhoods are relatively small geographic units with a relatively small and well defined population. As a result, "rational" individuals are likely to determine that their participation in the neighborhood civic association's activities will have a significant impact on its ability to achieve its collective goals. However, most neighborhood civic associations are not in a position to offer material benefits. As a result, their formation and survival are largely dependent on solidary and purposive incentives.

Scholars of interest group formation suggest that when an interest group is not in a position to offer its potential members material incentives, the organization's formation is largely dependent on the efforts of an organizational entrepreneur who is willing to shoulder the burdens of organizational management (Salisbury 1969; Schlozman and Tierney 1986). Since organizational entrepreneurs are relatively scarce, it is not so surprising that many neighborhoods experiencing decline or facing other difficulties have not formed into neighborhood civic associations. The free rider problem also helps explain why neighborhood activists often find it difficult to keep the neighborhood's residents involved in the association's activities after it has started up. Most neighborhood civic associations are relatively short-lived because the neighborhood's residents recognize that they can enjoy the benefits of any improvement efforts that might arise, even if they do not share the burden of attending meetings, writing, calling, or meeting with their local government officials, or any of the other time-consuming activities that are necessary to keep the association going. Often, when the neighborhood's spokesperson (organizational entrepreneur) moves from the neighborhood or quits the association, it dissolves (Frazier 1989).

Because of the free rider problem, even those who advocate the use of neighborhood civic associations as a mechanism to supplement local government efforts to improve the plight of the poor recognize that they have severe organizational limitations. As one author has argued, the physical and social collapse of many neighborhoods reflects the absence of powerful self-help mechanisms. Although voluntary block watches and clean-up/fix-up efforts can be exceptionally cost effective, they have seldom proven to be durable over time. Efforts by governmental agencies are more permanent, but they have proven to be expensive, and have done little to generate lasting improvements. As a result, that author concluded that the solution to solving the problem of urban blight is to generate powerful self-help mechanisms at the neighborhood level that are not subject to the free rider problem. In short, his solution to urban blight is the formation of RCAs in these areas (Frazier 1989).

RCAs and the Free Rider Problem

RCAs are less likely to suffer from the free rider problem than neighborhood civic associations because RCA membership is not voluntary and RCAs offer their members material benefits. Because RCA members are subject to the covenants attached to their property deeds, all property owners in an RCA-governed neighborhood agree, by purchasing their property, to share in the burden of improving the living and working conditions in the neighborhood. This is done, at the minimum, by adhering to the neighborhood's covenants and paying the neighborhood's assessment fees which, in turn, are used to provide goods and services that enhance the neighborhood's aesthetics and quality of life. Beyond that, neighbors can volunteer their time to serve as a member of their RCA's board of directors or on one of its committees or task forces. Since RCAs provide material benefits to their members and determine the assessment fees that pay for these benefits, RCA members have an economic incentive to participate. However, RCAs are not totally exempt from the free rider problem. The presence of material benefits alone does not guarantee that all RCA members will participate.

A RCA's effectiveness as a mechanism to improve the neighborhood's quality of life depends, at least in part, on the willingness of its members to volunteer their time and expertise to assist the RCA in carrying out its functions. As discussed in Chapter 5, RCA members have rarely refused to pay their assessments and there are legal mechanisms in place to assure compliance with the association's covenants. However, it is not uncommon for many RCAs to have a very difficult time getting members to become actively involved in its activities. As a recent California study documented, many of the smaller RCAs there routinely had vacancies on their board of directors because they could not find enough people who were willing to serve on the board (Barton and Silverman 1987a). Moreover, many RCAs report difficulties in generating a quorum at their annual or semi-annual general membership meetings. Most RCA bylaws set a quorum as a majority of the membership. Since relatively few RCAs have been able to achieve a quorum at their general meetings, most now allow proxy voting so that they can complete their business. Other RCAs have resorted to offering entertainment, meals, or prizes to lure members to the meetings (Brooks 1990a). This reluctance on the part of RCA members to volunteer to serve on the board of directors, on one of their RCA's committees or task forces, or to even attend its general membership meetings is caused, at least in part, by the members' recognition that they can often enjoy the benefits of their RCA's activities without becoming personally involved in them.

RCAs as Neighborhood Advocates

Like voluntary neighborhood civic associations, RCAs are designed to represent the interests of their members. Since local governments directly affect the welfare of RCA members through their taxing, zoning, and service delivery functions, it would be reasonable to assume that RCAs attempt to influence the outcome of local government decisions, particularly those that directly affect the neighborhood. It would also be reasonable to assume that since voluntary neighborhood civic associations have proven to be effective lobbying organizations at the local government level that RCAs would also be effective at lobbying local governments because RCAs have several organizational advantages over neighborhood civic associations. These advantages include less of a problem with free riders, the ability to raise revenue through assessment fees that can be used to purchase the services of lawyers, planners, and other professionals to assist them in their lobbying efforts, neighbors who are accustomed to attending neighborhood meetings to discuss issues affecting the neighborhood, and established newsletters that can be used to communicate issues of concern and plans of action.

Newspaper accounts of RCAs activities substantiate these assumptions. Articles appearing in the nation's leading newspapers during the latter half of the 1980s indicate that RCAs regularly lobby local government officials, are very effective in altering local governmental decisions, and are capable of extracting significant concessions from developers and others proposing physical change in and around their neighborhoods. These articles also indicate that RCA board members, especially in urban areas, are regular participants at city council and county supervisors' meetings. Complaining about urban encroachment and undesirable development in surrounding areas, they are as much a part of the NIMBY movement as are neighborhood civic associations (Vesey 1983; Marchese 1987; Hornblower 1988). Newspaper accounts of RCAs' interaction with local government officials suggest that the relationship between them is marked by conflict and confrontation. According to these reports, RCAs routinely lobby city and county officials on a personal basis and set aside a portion of the association's assessments to hire attorneys, engineers, planners, and other professionals to present their case. If it appears that those officials are going to make a decision that is perceived to adversely affect the neighborhood, newspaper accounts suggest that RCAs are more than willing to turn to more aggressive forms of persuasion, such as marching on city hall and running advertisements in the local newspaper that attack those policymakers who oppose the neighborhood's position.

Newspaper accounts suggest that RCAs are powerful and influential lobbying organizations at the local level. Their lobbying efforts are of interest because RCAs generally do not appear in the literature on state and local government, urban affairs, or interest groups. As such, there is an intrinsic academic interest in examining RCAs' lobbying efforts to determine their resources, methods of persuasion, and the effectiveness of their efforts. Moreover, since most RCAs represent the interests of homeowners in middle to upper-middle income groups and one of their primary political objectives appears to be preventing the location of adverse developments near their neighborhoods, there is also an interest in determining where these adverse developments are ultimately located. It may be that RCAs are using their influence to push these adverse developments onto poorer neighborhoods, that they are preventing these developments from occurring at all, that they are convincing local governments to enact mitigating conditions to reduce the adverse impact of these developments on their neighborhood, or that they are responsible for a combination of all of the above. At least one scholar (Frank Popper, chairman of urban studies at Rutgers University) has blamed the NIMBY movement for paralyzing the nation, claiming that it (i.e., RCAs and voluntary neighborhood civic associations) has been primarily responsible for preventing the placement of needed hazardous-waste sites, major metropolitan airports, and prisons (Hornblower 1988).

Unfortunately, there has been very little academic research on the interaction between RCAs and local governments. As a result, the behavioral model suggested by press accounts has not been either substantiated or refuted. However, the research that has been done suggests that newspaper accounts may overdramatize the influence and scope of RCA political activities.

Barton and Silverman's California Study

In 1986, Stephen Barton and Carol Silverman conducted an in-depth study of RCAs in California. Among the issues they explored was the general relationship that exists between RCAs and local government officials. Although their study did not focus on the specific ways RCAs and local government officials interact, they concluded that RCAs there did not show a major interest in local government affairs. Most of the RCAs they examined purposively avoided taking stands on any electoral issues that did not directly affect their neighborhood on the grounds that this was the prerogative of the individual voter and that conflict over such issues would disrupt the working relationships within the association. In addition, they discovered that very few RCAs had governmental affairs committees and the ones that did usually had only a single member on the committee who had a personal desire to be involved in local political affairs. RCA involvement with local government officials, they concluded, was sporadic and limited to zoning and permit issues that had an immediate impact on the neighborhood. As a result, they argued that RCAs are far more self-enclosed than voluntary neighborhood civic associations and that mandatory membership in RCAs seemed to depoliticize the association (Barton and Silverman 1987a).

ACIR's National Survey

In 1988, the U.S. Advisory Commission on Intergovernmental Relations (ACIR) conducted a nationwide survey of RCA board members that was designed to provide information on how RCAs affect the intergovernmental system of governance. One of the areas that ACIR was interested in knowing more about was the relationship that exists between RCAs and local governments.

ACIR's survey was not designed to determine the extent of RCA's lobbying resources or the specific methods of persuasion they employ to influence local government decisions. However, it did ask RCA board members to evaluate their overall relationship with their local government officials, to indicate how often they interacted with them, and to specify what issues were discussed.

ACIR's survey results suggested that RCAs generally have a cooperative, positive relationship with their local government officials, although there was evidence of an undercurrent of discontent. Specifically, RCA board members were asked to respond to two questions that were designed to evaluate their overall relationship with their local government. First, the board members were asked to rate the level of cooperation that exists between their RCA and their local government. Respondents could choose either excellent, good, fair, or poor. If newspaper accounts were to be believed, it would be expected that a majority of the respondents would have indicated that the level of cooperation was only fair or poor. However, a majority of the respondents (56%) indicated that they would rate the level of cooperation between their RCA and local government as either excellent (16%) or good (39%). Still, one out of every three RCA board members did rate the level of cooperation between themselves and their local government as only fair (23%) or poor (10%). Another 11 percent indicated either no contact (6%), don't know (1%), or failed to answer the question (5%). ACIR concluded that the results of the cooperation question suggested that there was a sizable undercurrent of dissatisfaction among RCA board members concerning their relationship with local government officials.

ACIR also asked RCA board members to rate the fairness of their local government regarding a series of specific government activities, including police protection, traffic, parks and recreation, location of traffic signals and stop signs, schools, animal control, zoning, and parking. Respondents could choose among very fair, somewhat fair, somewhat unfair, and very unfair. Again, if newspaper accounts were to be believed, it would be expected that a majority of the respondents would have rated their local government as being either somewhat unfair or very unfair on a majority of the services listed in the survey. However, a majority of respondents rated their local government as being either very fair or somewhat fair on all of the specific governmental activities included in the survey. The activity rated most highly for fairness was police protection (71% of the respondents indicated either very fair or somewhat fair) and the activity regarded as the least fair was local government taxes (30% of the respondents indicated that local taxes were either somewhat unfair or very unfair). Once again, a strong undercurrent of discontent concerning local government relations was in evidence as nearly every service listed in the survey had between 15 and 20 percent of the respondents who described their local government as being very unfair (ACIR 1989).

ACIR's survey results also suggested that the scope and intensity of RCAs' lobbying efforts is fairly limited. Specifically, RCA board members were asked if their RCA had attempted to influence local government officials with regard to 13 public services. As Table 6.1 indicates, the most common response by RCA board members was that their RCA had not attempted to influence their local government with regard to each of the specific services mentioned.

The typical RCA reported an attempt to influence local government on 3.7 of the 13 listed services, with police protection and the location of stop signs and traffic lights being the issues most frequently discussed. Homeowners' associations reported slightly more contacts with their local government officials (an average of 4.3 services) than condominium associations (an average of 3.2 services). Homeowners' associations were more likely than condominium associations to contact their local government officials about the issues of development/growth, location of traffic signals and stop signs, animal control, and schools.

Although ACIR's investigators did not attempt to determine

Table 6.1
1988 ACIR Survey: Has Your RCA Attempted to Influence Your Local Government? with Regard to . . .

Specific Service	*Percent Indicating Yes*
Police protection	48%
Locating stop signs/traffic lights	41
Traffic patterns around the neighborhood	35
Development/growth	33
Parking	32
Traffic patterns through the neighborhood	32
Zoning	30
Animal control	24
Water/sewer	23
Local government taxes	23
Environmental pollution	18
Parks/recreation	17
Schools	13

Source: U.S. Advisory Commission on Intergovernmental Relations. 1989. *Residential Community Associations: Private Governments in the Intergovernmental System?* Washington, DC: ACIR.

why homeowners' associations were more likely than condominium associations to interact with local government officials, they did speculate that the lifestyle differences that exist between the two RCA types may be a factor. The typical homeowners' association member is much more likely to have children than the typical condominium association member. For the most part, condominium associations are much more likely to have a membership primarily composed of single people and childless couples. Thus, school issues and, to a lesser extent, animal control issues are more likely to be a concern in homeowners' associations than in condominium associations (ACIR 1989).

The ACIR survey also attempted to determine the extent to which local government officials contacted RCA board members. Specifically, they asked RCA board members if their local government had attempted to influence their RCA with regard to the aforementioned 13 public services. The most common response was that their local government had not attempted to influence them with regard to each of the specific services mentioned. As Table 6.2 indicates, the frequency distribution ranged from a high

Table 6.2
1988 ACIR Survey: Has Your Local Government Attempted to Influence Your RCA? with Regard to . . .

Specific Service	*Percent Indicating Yes*
Police protection	14%
Water/sewer	14
Traffic patterns around the neighborhood	13
Zoning	13
Development/growth	13
Locating stop signs/traffic lights	11
Traffic patterns through the neighborhood	11
Environmental pollution	9
Local government taxes	9
Parks/recreation	8
Parking	8
Schools	6
Animal control	5

Source: U.S. Advisory Commission on Intergovernmental Relations. 1989. *Residential Community Associations: Private Governments in the Intergovernmental System?* Washington, DC: ACIR.

of only 14 percent for police protection and water/sewer services to a low of 5 percent for animal control.

ACIR's investigators concluded from the responses to the two questions concerning the frequency and direction of RCA/local government contacts that although RCA board members will not hesitate to let their local officials know their views when police protection is perceived to be wanting, or when local development, traffic patterns, or zoning decisions are perceived to jeopardize their quality of life or property values, these problems occurred relatively infrequently. As a result, ACIR concluded that RCAs have relatively few contacts with local government officials and when they do, the initial contact is usually made by the RCA. The report indicated that the prevailing attitude among RCA board members concerning their local government officials is "we leave them alone, and they leave us alone" (ACIR 1989).

Unfortunately, ACIR's survey did not indicate a time frame when it asked respondents to indicate if they had attempted to influence their local government officials or if their local government officials had attempted to influence them on the 13 listed services. As a result, it is not known if their responses refer to events within the preceding year, over the last decade, or even longer. If the responses refer to events that took place during the preceding year, it could be argued that RCAs are fairly active when it comes to lobbying local government officials. If the responses refer to events that have taken place since the RCA's formation, then ACIR's conclusion that RCAs do not have very frequent contact with local government officials would have been strengthened. In addition, ACIR's investigators indicated that their conclusions concerning RCA's lobbying activities had to be considered tentative because they had neglected to include trash collection as an issue in its survey. Since trash collection is widely recognized as one of the issues most frequently discussed by RCA board members with local government officials, ACIR's investigators indicated that their findings probably understate the extent and frequency of RCAs' attempts to influence local government officials (ACIR 1989).

The authors of ACIR's survey concluded their report by arguing that the relationship between local governments and RCAs is generally positive. Most RCA board members believe that their local government treats their association fairly and is willing to cooperate with their RCA. However, they also noted that a strong undercurrent of discontent with local government exists. It is highly likely that newspaper accounts of RCA political activities are a reflection of this undercurrent of discontent.

1990 National Survey

Using ACIR's survey as a starting point, and with the assistance of the Community Associations Institute (CAI), a second nationwide survey of RCA board members was conducted by this author in 1990. Like ACIR's survey, the 1990 survey was designed to further the understanding of RCAs' role in supplying services that are traditionally provided by local governments. Unlike ACIR's survey, the 1990 survey was designed specifically to determine the extent and nature of RCA's lobbying efforts.

The 1990 survey was mailed to 1,100 RCAs randomly selected from the Community Associations Institute's membership list. A total of 561 surveys were returned for a response rate of 51 percent. Like ACIR's survey, the data reported here refer to RCAs with the following characteristics:

- The organization is territorial in scope. That is, it encompasses a plot of land, including buildings, open spaces, and parking lots, and has defined boundaries, much like a municipality.
- The covenants creating the community association include mandatory membership and mandatory fees for home or lot owners, as well as rules governing resident behavior, particularly with regard to the exterior characteristics of residences.
- The organization is responsible for the regulation and management of common areas and the provision of services such as maintenance of recreational areas and facilities, parking lots, streets, and sidewalks.

In addition, like ACIR's survey results, the results of the 1990 survey may be biased because both used CAI's membership list to generate their random samples. Although the CAI's membership list is the most comprehensive list of RCAs available, analysts at

CAI admit that it is not fully representative of RCAs nationwide. First, they admit that they have not been very successful in getting RCAs located in New York to join their organization. In addition, because membership in the CAI requires the payment of dues, larger RCAs are more likely than smaller RCAs to join. As a result, the survey results may not fully represent the views of smaller RCAs and of those located in New York.

Recognizing that the 1990 survey's random sample was drawn from CAI's membership list, that their list had some built-in biases, and that the representativeness of the survey's respondents may be challenged, the survey included a series of demographic questions that were designed to determine if the respondents had attributes similar to those believed to exist among RCAs nationwide. Specifically, the respondents were asked questions concerning their RCA's location, type, composition, and extent of services.

The location of the respondents to the 1990 survey were representative of what is known about the location of RCAs nationwide. Specifically, 62 percent of the 1990 survey's respondents were located in suburban areas, 30 percent in urban areas, and 8 percent in rural areas. In addition, respondents were distributed geographically across the United States in roughly the same proportion known to exist among RCAs nationwide (17% in the Northeast, 26% in the South, 13% in the Midwest, and 44% in the West). The largest number of respondents were located in California, Virginia, Florida, New Jersey, Maryland, and Texas.

The type of RCA responding to the 1990 survey was also representative of what is known about the types of RCAs existing nationwide. Specifically, a majority of the 1990 survey's respondents were board members of condominium associations (61%), followed by board members of homeowners' associations (35%) and by board members of cooperatives and others (4%).

The composition of the RCAs responding to the 1990 survey was also representative of what is known about the composition of RCAs existing nationwide. Thirty-six percent of the respondents' RCAs were composed primarily of single-family townhouses or duplexes, 22 percent of 3 to 5 story multi-unit, multi-family buildings, 17 percent of single-family detached houses, 13 percent of high-rise buildings over 5 stories, and the remainder, 12 percent, either did not respond to the question or listed a combination of several different building types.

The number of services provided by the respondents' RCAs also were representative of the wide diversity known to exist among RCAs nationally. As indicated in Table 2.3, the number of services offered by the respondents' RCAs varied from 1 to 19, with the mode being 12 services (65 respondents) and the mean being 10 services. Most of the respondents' RCAs offered between 4 and 14 services.

Since the respondents to the 1990 survey had demographic characteristics that mirrored the characteristics believed to exist among RCAs nationwide, the concern that the 1990 survey results may have serious built-in biases was dispelled. The random sample drawn from CAI's membership list appears to be fairly representative of RCAs nationwide.

Like ACIR's survey, the 1990 survey asked respondents to rate their RCA's relationship with local government officials. Sixteen percent of the respondents indicated that their RCA's relationship with their local government was excellent, 46 percent indicated that it was good, 15 percent said fair, 4 percent said poor, and 19 percent indicated that they had no relationship with their local government.

The response to this question was very similar to the response ACIR's investigators received in their 1988 survey. A majority of the respondents in both surveys indicated that they would rate the relationship between their RCA and local government as either excellent or good. However, both surveys also revealed that there is a sizable undercurrent of dissatisfaction among RCA board members concerning their relationship with local government officials.

The 1990 survey also asked RCA board members a series of questions designed to determine the scope and intensity of their efforts to influence local government decisionmakers. Specifically, they were asked if anyone from their association had attended a local government meeting on behalf of the association during the past year, if anyone from their association had spoken or written to a local government official on behalf of the association during the past year, what issues were discussed if someone had spoken or written to a local government official during the past year, and if the association had ever endorsed a political candidate or sponsored a political candidate's forum.

The responses to these questions suggest that while RCAs' lobbying efforts are clearly a secondary function for most RCAs, they are more active in the political arena than either the ACIR's survey or Barton and Silverman's study suggested. Seventy percent of the RCA board members who responded to the 1990 survey indicated that they regularly monitored local government actions and 63 percent indicated that they had personally attended at least one local government meeting on behalf of their RCA in the past year. Moreover, 78 percent of the respondents indicated that someone from their RCA had either called or written to a local government official on behalf of the association during the past year. The number of issues discussed ranged from 1 to 10, with the most frequently cited number of issues discussed during the past year (1989) being 2. Traffic led the list of issues discussed (161 respondents) followed by zoning concerns, police protection, development issues, water and sewer services, and trash collection (see Table 2.4, for details).

These results suggest that RCAs routinely monitor local government decisions and provide input to local government decisionmakers when they perceive that the associations' interests may be adversely affected by a pending local government decision. The results also suggest that the relationship between RCAs and their local governments is not necessarily marked by conflict and confrontation. The vast majority of RCAs engage in what has been referred to in the interest group literature as an insider's or direct lobbying strategy, where the emphasis is on cultivating a good, personal relationship with government policymakers, monitoring their activities, and providing them with the organization's views when an issue arises that affects them.

The primary goal of the insider's lobbying strategy is to create an atmosphere of mutual trust where the lobbying organization is afforded an opportunity by policymakers to provide input into the policymaking system early in the decisionmaking process. In this way, the lobbying organization can either prevent or mitigate any actions that may have an adverse impact on them before they gain momentum (Schlozman and Tierney 1986).

Lobbying organizations that either cannot pursue the insider's lobbying strategy or discover that their insider's strategy has failed, will often engage in what has been referred to as the outsider's or indirect lobbying strategy. Of course, some lobbying organizations pursue both the insider's and outsider's strategies simultaneously.

The primary goal of the outsider's strategy is to bring political pressure to bear on policymakers to either prevent or mitigate the impact of their decisions on the organization's constituency. It focuses on more confrontational political activities than the insider's strategy. Examples would be marching on city hall, picketing development sites, and endorsing or opposing specific local government candidates in an effort to arouse the policymaker's constituency to his or her shortcomings. Although newspaper accounts suggest that RCAs regularly employ the outsider's strategy, most RCAs do not engage in these activities. When asked about their RCA's political activities, only 8 percent of the survey's respondents indicated that their RCA had ever sponsored a political candidates' forum and only 4 percent responded that their association had ever endorsed a political candidate.

Although relatively few RCAs engage in the outsider's strategy, there is anecdotal evidence that RCAs are increasingly engaging in political action that transcends their local lobbying efforts. In Boston, the Greater Boston Area Association of RCA presidents was formed to lobby local government officials for increased public services and has become involved in local political elections there (ACIR 1989). In New Jersey, RCA members recently embarked on an extensive letter writing campaign that resulted in their state government enacting the nation's first statewide legislation mandating local government reimbursement to RCAs for the provision of public services. In this case, the state law mandates RCA reimbursement for snow and ice removal, street lighting, and collection of leaves, recyclables, and garbage (Krugh 1990). Similar letter writing campaigns are expected to be launched throughout the nation over the next several years.

The implications of RCAs' involvement in local politics have not been fully explored and represent a major new area for scholarly attention. In states with weak party organizations at the local level they may serve to fill an organizational void and act as the primary vehicle for promoting participation in local politics. In states with strong party organizations at the local level, they may serve as important alternative vehicles for promoting local political participation. As such, they may augment the prospects for a pluralist society.

In an effort to determine if RCAs facilitate local political participation, the 1990 survey asked RCA board members to indicate if they or their RCA's members were more likely to monitor local government actions, attend a local government meeting, work on behalf of a candidate for local political office, work for a local political party organization, seek appointment to a government board or commission, or run for political office as a result of their experiences with their RCA. Their responses indicate that RCAs do encourage, to a limited extent, participation in local political affairs. Specifically, 65 percent of the respondents indicated that they were more likely to monitor local government actions, 57 percent indicated that they were more likely to attend a local government meeting, 14 percent indicated that they were more likely to work on behalf of a candidate for local political office, 8 percent indicated that they were more likely to work for a local political party organization, 17 percent indicated that they were more likely to seek appointment to a government board or commission, and 5 percent indicated that they were more likely to run for political office as a result of their experiences with their RCA. In addition, 60 percent of the respondents thought that their RCA's members were more likely to monitor local government actions, 50 percent believed that they were more likely to attend a local government meeting, 13 percent were convinced that they were more likely to work on behalf of a candidate for local political office, 7 percent indicated that they were more likely to work for a local political party organization, 8 percent responded that they were more likely to seek appointment to a government board or commission, and 4 percent noted that they were more likely to run for political office as a result of their experiences with their RCA (Dilger 1990).

Although the response to these questions suggests that RCAs do, at least to a small degree, encourage participation in local political affairs, Barton and Silverman's study of California's RCAs, ACIR's survey, and the 1990 survey all suggest that RCA lobbying and local electoral activities are focused on specific issues that affect their particular neighborhood such as trash collection, zoning, police protection, and tax equity issues. As a result, RCA's role as a facilitator of local political participation is muted and is not likely to be a significant factor in most cities and counties.

There is anecdotal evidence that RCAs may be serving as important new incubators for political organizers and, to a lesser extent, for local political candidates (Kleine 1989). RCA board members know their neighborhoods and have ready access to names and telephone numbers. They are also among the opinion leaders in their neighborhood and regularly meet with presidents and board members of other organizations such as the P.T.A. and Little League. As such, local political candidates are increasingly turning to RCA leaders to serve as precinct captains and to head neighborhood get-out-the-vote efforts. There is also anecdotal evidence that increasing numbers of RCA board members are either considering or have actually run for local political office. However, their responsibility for enforcing neighborhood CC&Rs often cause them to develop enemies as well as friends in their neighborhood, weakening the value of the election to a RCA-governing board post as a springboard to local elective office (Barton and Silverman 1989).

In summary, the 1990 survey results suggest that while many RCA board members may prefer to have what the ACIR report referred to as a "we leave them alone and they leave us alone" relationship with their local government, most recognize the potential influence of local government decisions on their neighborhood and have an ongoing, if somewhat wary, relationship with their local government.

RCAs as a Lobbying Force

Newspaper accounts of RCAs' lobbying activities at the local government level indicate that RCAs can be very influential lobbying organizations. Through their assessment powers they have the capacity to raise significant amounts of revenue that can be used to hire professional lobbying assistance, including attorneys, engineers, and planners. In addition, they already have in place, through their association's newsletter, a communications network that can be used to mobilize the neighborhood for political action. Moreover, the board of directors constitutes a ready-made forum for providing the political leadership that is often necessary to serve as a catalyst for neighborhood political action. In short, RCAs are a potent, but latent lobbying power at the local level. In some ways RCAs are like sleeping tigers. When left alone, they are of little concern to those around them, but once aroused from their sleep, they are clearly a force to be reckoned with at the local government level.

7

RCAs and Civic Virtue

As indicated in Chapter 5, RCAs' advocates applaud the emergence of RCAs primarily because they are convinced that RCAs can provide services more efficiently than government and are generally more responsive than government to citizen's desires. In their view, government has relatively few incentives to economize or respond to taxpayers' desires because, like monopolies in the private sector, it has no competitors. Moreover, taxpayers are required to pay for the government's services regardless of its performance as a service provider and even if they do not want the services (Frazier 1985). In contrast, the relatively intimate nature of RCA governance creates strong incentives for board members to economize and be responsive to the RCA's members' desires for services. As Robert Ellickson, a professor at Stanford University's Law School has argued:

> . . . There's no question that [RCAs] are faster and cheaper [than government]. The incentives are stronger in the private sector. People can coordinate with one another more than is generally recognized (Garreau 1987).

Another important, and often overlooked, reason RCAs' advocates applaud the emergence of RCAs is that they view them as vehicles for providing people of similar backgrounds and values an opportunity to join together to create a strong sense of community at the local level. They suggest that in contrast to government, which is often remote and bureaucratic, RCAs offer an opportunity for direct democracy where neighbors meet face to face to resolve their common problems. This interaction, they argue, promotes a stronger sense of civic virtue (defined in terms of RCA members' participation, communication, and involvement in collective decisionmaking) because neighbors recognize the efficacy of their participation in RCA meetings. As one of the leading advocates of RCAs has argued, unlike local governments, RCAs provide citizens an opportunity to participate directly, at a more manageable scale, in the governance of their local neighborhood and community. This participation, in turn, can and should support the basic goals of government regarding participation, communication, and involvement of its citizens in local decisionmaking (Dowden 1980).

Direct Democracy and Civic Virtue

There is a strong and prevailing belief embedded in the American political culture that direct, participatory democracy is the best governmental form because its decisionmaking process is based clearly and directly on the consent of the governed. As a result, Americans have always valued citizen participation in public affairs. However, there has also been a recognition that in a nation as large as the United States that direct, participatory democracy, in most instances, is not a viable option (Thompson 1970). We value democracy, but recognize that the republican form of governance is a more practical, if somewhat less precise, means of securing a public decisionmaking process that is based on the consent of the governed. This may help to explain, at least in part, why Americans insist that they live in a democracy when they do not, why they lament any decline in voter turnout in presidential and congressional elections, and why they are fascinated with and appreciate the New England town meeting as a public decisionmaking authority (Mansbridge 1980; Gans 1989; Pierson 1989). It also helps to explain why some advocate the formation of RCAs.

Many of RCA's advocates view RCAs as a means to provide citizens a relatively rare opportunity to participate directly in public decisions. In their view, participation in RCA governance promotes a broader sense of civic virtue and legitimacy for the political process as neighbors become accustomed to thinking about public issues and recognize their own role in promoting the collective good for their neighborhood. Their argument is reminiscent of Alexis de Tocqueville's who suggested that decentralizing important public policy decisions encouraged citizens to participate in political affairs because they can readily see the consequences of those decisions on their lives. He argued that political participation and decentralization of authority worked hand-in-hand to prevent democratic despotism by creating a political environment that encouraged the American people to view government not as a means of exploiting others and furthering their own self-interest but as a means to promote the public interest (Tocqueville 1840; Heffner 1956; Diamond 1974). Similarly, RCAs' advocates argue that participation in RCA governance creates a public-spiritedness among its members that spills over into other aspects of their lives. Specifically, they suggest that RCAs encourage people to become more knowledgeable about local political affairs, to participate in local government decisionmaking, and to view the world not in terms of their own narrow self-interest but the broader interests of their neighborhood. As a result, RCAs, at least to a small extent, help to bring about a more just society because they serve to empower individuals who would otherwise not provide their input into the political process. Moreover, recent research has suggested that even when citizens are displeased with the outcomes of their interactions with authority figures and institutions they will accept those outcomes as legitimate if they are provided an opportunity to present their views before the final decision has been reached and if the decisionmakers are perceived to be impartial (Tyler, Casper, and Fisher 1989). As a result, if RCAs do promote civic virtue and participation in local political affairs then, even when their members are not pleased with the outcome of their efforts, RCAs may also serve to augment citizen perceptions of governmental institutions as being legitimate and worthy of their support. However, the assertion that RCAs promote civic virtue and participation in local political affairs has never been tested.

RCAs and Civic Virtue: 1990 Survey Results

Although political theorists continue to disagree over the role that public participation and civic virtue play in the creation and maintenance of a legitimate and just society, and many political theorists during the twentieth century have questioned the capacity of most citizens to fully comprehend the complex decisions that face governments in the modern era, with only a few exceptions they agree that institutions that encourage people to become more informed about political issues and participate constructively in political life should be encouraged and praised (Thompson 1970; ACIR 1980). However, the evidence concerning RCA's impact on political participation and civic virtue is mixed. Newspaper accounts of RCA's lobbying efforts and surveys of RCA interactions with local government officials suggest that it can be argued, on a case-by-case basis, that RCAs do heighten their members' awareness of some local political issues, particularly those involving development, zoning, and traffic patterns in and around their neighborhood. They also suggest that RCAs encourage their members to participate in local political activities when the neighborhood's interests are threatened by governmental action. Moreover, they also suggest that RCAs provide a political base for some to enter political life and that they do create, through regular general membership and board of directors meetings, an additional arena for political interaction and involvement in collective decision-making (Marchese 1987; ACIR 1988; Dean 1989; Brooks 1990c, 1990d; Dilger 1990). Moreover, the 1990 survey of RCA board members revealed that they thought that participation in RCA governance did have some impact on their general membership's participation in and knowledge of local political affairs. Specifically, the survey asked RCA board members if they thought the general membership of their association was more likely to monitor government actions, attend a local government meeting, work on behalf of a candidate for local political office, work for a local political party organization, seek appointment to a government board or commission, or run for political office as a result of their experiences with their RCA. Sixty percent of the respondents indicated that they thought that their general membership was more likely to monitor government actions and 50 percent indicated that the general membership was more likely to attend a local government meeting as a result of their experiences with their RCA. In addition, 13 percent believed that their members were more likely to work on behalf of a candidate for local political office, 7 percent indicated that their members were more likely to work for a local political party organization, 8 percent felt that their members were more likely to seek appointment to a government board or commission, and 4 percent indicated that their members were more likely to run for political office as a result of their experiences with their RCA (Dilger 1990). However, most RCA board members also indicated that they did not view the enhancement of their members' participation in political affairs to be one of their RCA's primary functions. Most of them did not purposefully attempt, like an organized interest group, to enhance their membership's political awareness on a continuing basis. Instead, they focused their attention on providing services in a cost-effective manner and in enforcing the neighborhood's CC&Rs in a way that protects the neighborhood's aesthetics without making the board of directors appear to be arbitrary or capricious. Their role in fostering political awareness and involvement in local governmental affairs usually arose only after they found out that government has taken an action or was considering an action that was perceived to adversely affect the neighborhood's property values or aesthetics. Typically, they acted like an early warning system for the neighborhood, monitoring their local government's behavior on behalf of their neighbors. As part of this monitoring process, some RCA board members indicated in an open comment section of the survey that they maintained personal contact with a few, selected government policymakers, typically members of the local government's city council or planning commission as well as a few of their local government's administrators, usually the city manager or planning director (Dilger 1990). As such, it can be argued that RCAs may play a relatively significant role as a facilitator of civic virtue among their board members, but their role as a facilitator of civic virtue for their general membership is relatively limited.

Some Questionable Assumptions

The 1990 survey results suggest that RCAs may serve, to a small extent and on a case-by-case basis, to augment local political awareness and activism among RCA members. However, their role as facilitators of civic virtue is muted because RCAs' internal decisionmaking processes and the attitudes and behavior of RCA members often differ significantly from the theoretical model suggested by RCAs' advocates. For example, most of those who advocate the formation of RCAs assume that RCAs follow accepted norms of decisionmaking that incorporate all the rights and privileges embodied in the U.S. Constitution, including the rights of free speech and assembly guaranteed in the First Amendment and the rights to due process and equal protection of under the law found in the Fourteenth Amendment. However, RCAs often employ decisionmaking processes that are far more closed and autocratic than those used by local government and mandated for all governments in the United States by the U.S. Constitution. In addition, RCA advocates also tend to assume that RCA members are genuinely interested in participating in their RCA's decisionmaking processes and are willing to work with other members of their RCA to foster their common interests. In their view, RCAs are models of what has been referred to as a unitary democracy. Unitary democracies are like friendships in that their decisionmaking processes are distinguished by a relatively high degree of common interest among their members, a shared desire to reach consensus, the importance placed on face-to-face negotiation and accommodation, and an emphasis on respect for the rights of others in the group. In unitary democracies the people reason together until they agree on the best answer. This contrasts with what has been referred to as adversary democracy which is more compatible with large-scale politics. Adversary democracies operate on the premise that there are competing interests among its members and that it is difficult, if not impossible, to reach consensus on most issues. As a result, there is little emphasis on face-to-face negotiation and accommodation. Instead, decisions are reached by a vote and the majority rules (Mansbridge 1980).

In many cases, RCAs fail to live up to the unitary democracy model. Although most RCA-governed communities are composed of individuals having relatively similar economic and social characteristics, they are not necessarily homogeneous communities of like minded homeowners working together in harmony to achieve their common goals. Instead, they have many tensions that result from the diversity of backgrounds and interests of their membership. For example, members with children are more likely to request that their RCA provide tot lots and playground equipment than members without children. Absentee homeowners who rent out their homes are more interested in keeping the RCA's assessment fees low than in having it provide additional services. Members who intend to sell their home soon tend to oppose assessment increases to build up reserves or fund major capital improvements such as street repaving while those who intend to stay in the neighborhood for a long time tend to support these assessments (Barton and Silverman 1989). Moreover, CC&R enforcement places major strains on the neighbor-helping-neighbor relationship that RCAs attempt to foster. This tension exists primarily because there is a tendency for homeowners to believe that they have inviolable rights to do whatever they want with their own home or in their own neighborhood. Evidence of these tensions has been documented by several surveys of RCA residents' attitudes and behavior. For example, a 1987 study of Florida condominiums concluded that conflicts and disputes among condominium residents and between residents and their condominium owners association were common. Most conflicts involved the enforcement of the association's CC&Rs, particularly those that limited the owner/resident's ability to make structural, landscaping, and interior design changes (Williamson and Adams 1987). In addition, a 1986 survey of RCA presidents located in California revealed that 27 percent had at least one member of their board of directors who had been harassed by another homeowner or subjected to personal accusations at a public meeting. A quarter of the RCA presidents surveyed also reported that they had been threatened with a lawsuit and 5 percent reported that they had been sued by members of their association during the preceding year. This was most likely to occur in larger RCAs primarily because their CC&Rs tend to be more extensive than smaller RCAs, increasing the likelihood of someone being cited with a violation. Also, larger RCAs typically provide more services than smaller RCAs, increasing the likelihood that someone in the RCA will become disenchanted with the association's performance (Barton and Silverman 1987a).

There have also been instances where RCA board members have been physically threatened by RCA members who had been cited for violating the association's CC&Rs. In Florida, an RCA president was threatened with a shotgun and another was bitten on the leg by a disgruntled homeowner. One condominium association even needed to post security guards at its board meetings to prevent fist fights. A resident there described the relationship between his board of directors and its members as being on a par with "the Hatfields and McCoys" (Winokur 1989b).

Newspaper accounts also suggest that RCAs may not be havens of participatory democracy. Newspapers regularly feature stories about RCAs that have become so embroiled in dispute that its members have not only sued their board of directors but each other as well. For example, disputes over blocked ocean views and architectural changes in 1988 among the members of the Spyglass Homeowners' Association in Corona del Mar, California, led to a recall election of the RCA's board of directors, lawsuits against the board of directors, and lawsuits among the association's members as well (Klein 1988).

Those who believe that RCAs promote civic virtue also tend to assume that when buyers purchase their homes in an RCA-governed neighborhood that they understand the role and powers of the RCAs' board of directors and their role and responsibilities as members of the RCA. However, many home buyers are not fully aware of these powers, the extent of the neighborhood's CC&Rs, the RCAs' financial condition, or the condition of the RCAs' common facilities when they purchase their homes. As an RCA advocate admitted, one of the most troublesome by-products of the sales process in RCA-governed neighborhoods are home buyers who subsequently claim that they were not advised before they purchased their home that there was an RCA, maintenance expenses, or CC&Rs governing their activities within the neighborhood. Although many developers now insist that home buyers sign a release indicating that they have received appropriate information concerning the RCA, its assessment fees, and its CC&Rs, industry representatives admit that these documents are seldom read and fully understood by most home buyers. There is also a problem with some overzealous sales personnel who move as quickly as possible to get the home buyer to settlement. Typically, there is no organized effort to educate the prospective buyer regarding the RCA and the rights and obligations that the buyer assumes when purchasing a home in an RCA-governed neighborhood. Moreover, the problem of misinformation is not limited to new sales within the RCA. Perhaps the greatest information problem arises in the case of resales where the original purchaser sells a home. Typically, the second buyer is provided with little or no information regarding the RCA and its CC&Rs (Dowden 1980). Currently, the burden is on the consumer to be informed about their obligations with regard to their community association. Only half the states require that condominium documents be disclosed to new purchasers, less than half require disclosure of condominium documents on resale of the home, and even fewer require disclosure of RCA documents for houses in planned residential developments (ACIR 1989).

Recognizing that many new home buyers in RCA-governed neighborhoods are not fully aware of their rights and obligations, nearly half of all RCAs surveyed in 1987 by the Community Associations Institute indicated that they furnished new residents with a welcome packet that typically included a welcome letter, general information on the RCA and its management, a copy of the association's CC&Rs, and important telephone numbers. In addition, 74 percent of the respondents indicated that they provided its members a neighborhood newsletter. Nearly half the newsletters were distributed monthly, 21 percent on a bi-monthly basis, and most of the remainder were distributed quarterly. The typical newsletter was between one and four pages long and, if a smaller RCA, was usually prepared by a board member or, if a larger RCA, by the RCA's manager (CAI Research Foundation 1987).

However, despite the distribution of welcome packets and newsletters, many RCA members remain ignorant of their RCA's operations because they react to their RCA's publications and internal politics in the same manner they react to political news and governmental politics: they do not pay much attention or actively participate in its decisionmaking processes unless its actions affects them directly and in an adverse way. For example, the California survey revealed that many RCAs there had a very difficult time obtaining a quorum at their general membership meetings. Thirty percent of the RCAs there could not obtain a quorum at their last general membership meeting even though most of them allowed proxy voting. The typical attendance at RCAs' general membership meetings in 1986 ranged between 25 and 50 percent of the membership. When asked to describe the amount of support they receive from their members, only 16 percent of the RCA presidents surveyed reported that they believed that their "members gave them a lot of support" while 39 percent said that their "members really don't care" (Barton and Silverman 1987b). Moreover, when asked to describe their association membership as being either "very involved," "participative," "apathetic," or "other," over half (53%) of the respondents to a nationwide survey of RCA board members conducted by the CAI Research Foundation in 1988 described their association members as being "apathetic" (Dale and McBee 1988).

The California survey not only suggested that many RCAs are subject to widespread apathy among their general membership but that they also have a very difficult time finding people who were willing to serve on their board of directors. Only 28 percent of the RCAs there reported that they had more candidates than seats in their last board election, 49 percent had the same number of candidates as seats, and 23 percent indicated that they could not find enough people willing to run to fill all available seats. Moreover, the survey revealed that fewer than 1 percent of RCA members had ever served on their board of directors or on any of its committees and that only 11 percent of RCA members had ever served in any voluntary capacity with their association. In addition, it discovered that a sizable minority of RCAs in California (19%) reported that one board member did all the association's work and an additional 3 percent had no one on the board or directors who had enough time to get things done. (Barton and Silverman 1989). The authors of the California survey concluded that getting the general membership interested in governing the association was one of the most difficult tasks facing RCAs there. In their view, their survey suggested that most RCA members typically rely on others to "take care of things" and only participate in their association's business when they feel threatened by its decisions or the actions of outsiders, such as a developer asking the local government to rezone land near their home or a government agency proposing a change in local traffic patterns. As a result, even after purchasing their homes in an RCA-governed neighborhood, many RCA members remain ignorant of the role and powers of their RCA's board of directors and either do not fully understand or do not care enough to learn about their role and responsibilities as members of the RCA (Barton and Silverman 1987a).

RCAs' Governing Structures

Many RCAs, particularly those with more than 100 units, are incorporated and in some jurisdictions, such as Florida, condominium associations must be incorporated. Obviously, any RCA that is incorporated is subject to corporate law (see Chapter 2 concerning the application of the business judgment rule and the fiduciary responsibility of RCA board members and officers). Moreover, because RCAs of all sizes have business responsibilities that involve numerous duties including the upkeep of common property, the preparation and maintenance of budgets and records, and the assessment of owners' shares of common expenses, most state courts have held unincorporated RCAs to the same legal standards as incorporated associations (Rosenberry 1985). More important, the courts have in most instances dealt with RCAs as if they were private, nonprofit mutual benefit corporations, not governmental entities. This legal distinction has important consequences for determining the legal standards applied to RCAs' governing structures. It may also help to explain why many RCA members do not participate in RCA governance and why RCAs' impact on civic virtue is not as profound as their advocates would claim.

Recognizing that RCAs have both business and governmental characteristics, state courts have ruled that RCAs' internal governance structures are not subject to the constitutional standards applied to government officials. However, they also have ruled that RCAs' operating rules and procedures must meet a higher legal standard than the one applied to businesses. RCAs' standard, referred to as the legal "rule of reasonableness," allows RCAs' internal rules and procedures to legally violate many constitutional edicts applied to government officials (Hyatt and Downer 1987; Hyatt 1988). For example, although RCAs may appear to represent the essence of local democracy and participation, voting privileges within most RCAs are based on home ownership rather than residence. Basing voting privileges on ownership originally came from the corporate model of governance where voting rights are granted to those who own stock in the company, not those who work for the company. In homeowners' associations, this has usually been manifested by the use of the one house, one vote principle where each home is assigned a single vote. The assumption is that each home benefits equally from the RCA's activities and has an equal stake in the RCA's decisions. Typically, the one house, one vote principle applies without regard to the type or mix of housing types in the homeowners' association. Each detached and attached home in a mixed use development is assigned an equal vote. Moreover, assessments within most homeowners' associations are also generally shared equally among the owners (Dowden 1986).

Condominium associations also base their voting rights on home ownership rather than on residence. However, because the nature of home ownership is different in condominium developments than in homeowner associations, some variations on the one house, one vote principle are often employed. If all the homes in the condominium association are basically the same size, then each home owns the same proportion of the total development and receives the same level of services from the association. In this case, the one house, one vote principle is typically employed. However, when the homes vary considerably in size and value, different allocation systems have been developed to provide a more equitable basis for allocating voting rights. Generally, the square footage of the condominium or the initial value or price of the condominium is used to weight votes within the RCA, providing those with larger, more valuable condominiums with more votes than those with smaller or less valuable homes. The variation is justified on the grounds that the home buyer is buying a percentage of the total development and is entitled to an equivalent percentage of the authority to determine what happens to the development. Typically, the same method that is employed to determine each owner's voting privileges within the condominium association is also employed to determine each owner's share of the association's expenses. Again, this is justified on the grounds that a homeowner who has purchased a certain percentage of the condominium development should pay that same percentage of the development's expenses (Dowden 1986).

By basing voting rights on home ownership rather than on residence, most RCAs disenfranchise renters. This is sometimes justified on the grounds that renters may oppose efforts to increase the neighborhood's property values because these efforts, if successful, could result in rent increases (ACIR 1988). Instead of allowing renters to vote, most RCAs give the home's absentee owners voting privileges within the association. As a result, investors who own more than one home in the association have more than one vote while many of the residences have none. This violates the principle of one person, one vote articulated in *Reynolds v. Sims* (1964), *Avery v. Midland County* (1968), and *Hadley v. Junior College District* (1970) for governmental entities and, for RCAs' detractors, harkens back to America's early days when the vote was reserved for white male property owners who were viewed as having the biggest stake in how the society was run (Garreau 1987).

The practice of basing suffrage on home ownership instead of residence affects the internal political dynamics of RCAs in a way that diminishes their capacity to act as facilitators of civic virtue. Disenfranchised renters have little incentive to participate in RCA governance and absentee owners are typically less interested in the RCAs' day-to-day operations than resident owners, less likely to actively engage in its governance structure and vote on association matters. In extreme cases, it is possible to have a RCA with a majority of its members who live outside the neighborhood and the neighborhood be composed of a majority of residents who are not members of the RCA (Barton and Silverman 1988). Under such circumstances, it is not surprising that relatively few residents get involved in RCA governance.

The constitutional principle of one person, one vote is further strained and the incentive to participate in RCA activities is further diminished when one or more absentee owners own a large number of the RCAs' homes and dominate its decisions (Barton and Silverman 1988). Moreover, since RCAs are not considered governmental entities, public sunshine and open meeting laws that apply to governmental meetings often do not apply and, because the courts do not consider them to be governmental bodies, the Fourteenth Amendment's due process of law clause does not apply to their internal operating procedures. Thus, depending on the particular state courts' finding concerning what is reasonable, RCA meetings may be held in secret and their decisionmaking processes may exclude resident homeowners and renters from having any input in decisions that affect them.

A recent survey conducted by the Community Associations Institute indicates that most RCAs do give notice of their meetings and most do open their meetings to all members and affected individuals for questions, comments, and suggestions. For example, 77 percent of the survey's respondents indicated that they provided an open-forum time at board meetings to give their members an opportunity to address the board and 90 percent indicated that their board meetings were open for observation by any member of their RCA. In addition, the survey revealed that the typical RCA held a general membership meeting twice a year. However, the survey also revealed that less than half of the responding RCAs had ever conducted a survey of their residents views and nearly three-quarters of the RCAs polled allocated less than 1 percent of their budget to communications programs with their members (CAI Research Foundation 1987).

The absence of mandatory sunshine and open meeting laws, the practice of basing voting privileges on ownership instead of residence, and the free rider induced reluctance of many home owners to participate in any governance process unless directly threatened may help to explain why RCA meetings are not always well attended and why homeowners and renters often resort to expensive and time-consuming litigation to remedy their claims against their RCA (Hyatt and Downer 1987; Hyatt 1988; and ACIR 1989).

8

Conclusions

The economic conditions that fostered the boom in RCA formation during the 1980s are still present. The market demand for condominiums and PUD housing continues to be strong, developers continue to view them as profitable economic ventures, and local governments continue to regard them as convenient and, in many instances, the only means available to pay for the infrastructure and service delivery costs that accompany residential development. As a result, it is very likely that the number of RCAs and the number of people subject to RCA governance will continue to grow exponentially throughout the 1990s and well into the next century. The Community Associations Institute's projection of 225,000 RCAs by the year 2000, with over 50 million persons subject to RCA governance, may turn out to be a conservative estimate (CAI 1988).

The debate over the desirability of creating PUDs and condominiums has focused primarily on the issues of housing marketability, developer profitability, and local government's budgetary considerations. Little attention has been paid to the impact their governing bodies have on the delivery of public services in the United States or their role in the broader debate over privatization and the related issues concerning whether it is better to centralize or decentralize decisionmaking authority in American society. Moreover, relatively little attention has been paid to the impact RCAs have on local government politics and elections, the political socialization of RCA members and their feelings toward government processes and political affairs, and ultimately, on the distribution of power in American society. As the number of RCAs continues to accelerate and the number of people subject to their governance continues to increase, these considerations are certain to play a more prominent role in the debate over the desirability of PUDs and condominiums in the years ahead.

The Delivery of Public Services

Although several studies have examined cities' experiences with the contracting out of services, no one has done a systematic evaluation of RCAs' experiences in this area. Surveys of RCA board members and the anecdotal evidence available suggests that most RCAs are providing services in a cost-efficient and effective manner.

Some have argued that load shedding governmental services to RCAs is a bad idea because many RCAs lack the economy of scale and the expertise to provide services more effectively and efficiently than government (Barton and Silverman 1987a, 1989). However, the 1990 nationwide survey of RCA board members indicated that 95 percent of them believed that their members would rate their RCA's performance as a service provider as either good or excellent. Moreover, over three-quarters of them (78%) indicated that there was not a single service currently being offered by their RCA that could be provided more efficiently by their local government (Dilger 1990).

It has also been suggested that local governments should not load shed services to RCAs because most residents and homeowners in RCA-governed communities find that the level of services, assessment fees, and covenants supplied and enforced by their RCA violate their expectations. This is evidenced by the relatively large and growing number of lawsuits that RCA members file annually against their RCA, by the lack of attendance at the general membership meetings, and by surveys of RCA officials which indicate that they are almost routinely subjected to personal harassment, open accusations, or the treat of a lawsuit by members of their RCA during the course of a typical year (Barton and Silverman 1987a; Winokur 1989b).

Although the number of lawsuits filed by RCA members against their RCA suggest that expectations are being violated, these lawsuits and much of the reported harassment of RCA officials frequently involve the enforcement of specific provisions in the RCA's CC&Rs that have little or nothing to do with RCAs' role as service providers. Typically, they involve disputes over controls of personal choices within a home, such as limiting the occupancy of a residence to a "traditionally defined" family, regulating interior space color schemes, and prescribing the age and childbearing practices of residents. If government required all RCAs to include provisions in their bylaws that allowed their members to revise their CC&Rs with less than unanimous consent (preferably by a two-thirds vote of the membership) and precluded controls over personal choices within the home that do not inflict harmful economic spillovers on the neighborhood, the amount of litigation filed annually by RCA members would probably drop significantly (Winokur 1989b; Korngold 1990). In addition, the increasing number of lawsuits filed annually by RCA members may not reflect growing dissatisfaction with RCAs. Instead, much of that increase may result from the expanded number of RCAs in existence and the increased number of people subject to RCA governance (Korngold 1990).

RCAs often have a difficult time in getting a majority of its members to attend their annual or biannual general membership meetings. However, this does not necessarily indicate widespread dissatisfaction with the performance of RCAs as service providers. Some of those not attending the meetings may stay at home because they are relatively satisfied with how the association is functioning and, as self-interested and rational free riders, let others do all the work while they enjoy the benefits of RCA membership. In addition, RCA member turnout at general membership meetings is higher than the turnout rate for all adults at local government elections and about the same as the turnout rate for registered voters at local government elections (Korngold 1990). Moreover, the difficulty of achieving a quorum at RCA general membership meetings may result from the unique dynamics of participatory democracy rather than from the dissatisfaction of its members. A comprehensive study of New England town meetings revealed that less than a majority of the adults there regularly attended their town meetings because the cost of personally attending and participating in general membership meetings is much greater than simply showing up at a voting booth and casting a ballot. The study suggested that attending a general membership meeting not only requires a much greater time commitment than casting a ballot but also involves much higher psychological costs, primarily involving the fear of speaking in public. Specifically, many New Englanders decided not to attend their town meeting because they feared that they might be made to look like a fool in front of neighbors, lose control of their temper and say something that they would later regret, or say something that will make an enemy out of a neighbor who they interact with on a regular and continuing basis (Mansbridge 1980). As a result, the relatively low turnout rates for RCA general membership meetings may not indicate widespread dissatisfaction with RCAs. Instead, they may reflect the relatively high costs of participating in an open meeting attended by people who are likely to know who you are and where you live.

Load shedding local government services to RCAs also raise many of the same issues that surround the controversy over the contracting out of local government services to private firms (see Chapter 4). For example, some economists have argued that contracting out and load shedding government services result in market efficiencies that will lead to a more robust economy. However, Keynesians worry that contracting out and load shedding government services will reduce the public sector's capacity to stabilize economic conditions. As a result, the evaluation of RCAs' desirability must include evaluations of their impact on the size of the public sector and the appropriate role of the public sector in regulating the American economy. Of course, there is little consensus over what the public sector's role in regulating the American economy ought to be. As a result, there is likely to be little consensus over the desirability of load shedding government services to RCAs or to any other entity.

Those who oppose contracting out and load shedding governmental services also argue that their cost savings are largely generated at the expense of public employees and unions. Although they have not directly addressed RCAs, they would likely argue that load shedding local government services to RCAs creates economic benefits for middle to upper income RCA members at the expense of lower income individuals who are denied the opportunity to compete for full-time public sector jobs that include paid benefits. Instead, they compete for jobs in the private sector that may or may not be full-time and may or may not include paid benefits. As a result, they would probably conclude that load shedding local government services to RCAs may result in more efficient markets, but it may not result in a more equitable society.

The introduction of equity considerations into the debate over the desirability of load shedding government services to RCAs raises severe methodological difficulties. The definition of what constitutes a more equitable society is based on value judgments that largely defy objective analysis. For example, the public sector has often led the way in the hiring of minorities. It can be argued on equity grounds that the public sector's role in promoting the economic fortunes of minorities should be considered as a plus for the public sector when evaluating the pros and cons of load shedding government services. However, it is impossible to quantify, in a precise way, what that plus is worth in economic terms. The importance of promoting the economic fortunes of minorities varies from individual to individual. As a result, one individual may argue that the public sector's role in promoting the economic fortunes of minorities is very important and very valuable, another may argue that it is only somewhat important and has only a little value, and still another may argue that it is not important and has no value. As a result, when equity considerations are brought into consideration it becomes extremely difficult to evaluate in an objective manner the appropriateness of load shedding local government services to RCAs or to any other entity. If your primary goal is to promote a more efficient society, then it is likely that you will generally approve of the formation of RCAs. If your primary goal is to promote a more equitable and fair society, than it is likely that you will be less impressed with RCAs performance as a service provider and will be more interested in determining their role in promoting a more pluralistic society.

Should Power Be Centralized or Decentralized?

Many of the same arguments presented in the debate concerning the role of the public and private sectors in decisionmaking and the appropriate authority of the national government versus the states and localities (see Chapter 4) can be applied to RCAs. For example, some analysts have argued that state and local governments cannot be trusted with power because they lack expertise, tend to be narrow-minded and parochial, and are structurally incapable of engaging in policies that redistribute from the rich to the poor (Henig 1985). RCAs have been accused of the same deficiencies (Barton and Silverman 1987a, 1989; Nelson 1989; Winokur 1989b). Moreover, RCAs' advocates use many of the same arguments used by those who advocate the decentralization of governmental power to state and local governments to defend the formation of RCAs. For example, RCAs advocates suggest that, like state and local governments, RCAs may have had problems in the past but have recently undergone structural transformations that have made them more effective, professional, and responsive to members' needs (Dowden 1980, 1986). In addition, like those who advocate the decentralization of power to state and local governments, RCAs advocates argue that there are advantages to reducing the scale of governance. They agree with state and local government advocates that state and local governments are better able than the national government to recognize and protect the diversity of values held by territorially defined groups. However, they are convinced that RCAs offer an even better organizational means to accomplish this goal. They also suggest that RCAs represent a very efficient organizational solution to meet the wide variations in preferences for public goods and services (Oakerson 1989b). Moreover, like Tocqueville, RCAs' advocates are convinced that it is necessary to decentralize important public policy decisions to the local level to promote feelings of political efficacy and legitimacy. If it is good to decentralize important public policy decisions to the local level, then they suggest that it is even better to decentralize important public policy decisions to the neighborhood level (Frazier 1984).

Of course, not everyone agrees that important public policy

decisions should be decentralized to the local government and neighborhood levels (see Chapter 4). Many have argued that it is neither necessary nor appropriate to recognize and protect the diversity of values in American society. Instead, they suggest that Americans should hold allegiance to the national interest as opposed to the more parochial state, local, or neighborhood interests. For example, they view the NIMBY movement as obstructing progress. In addition, they are convinced that the national government has both the right and the obligation to see that certain fundamental values are enforced throughout American society, such as the protection of civil rights and the care for the poor and the elderly. As a result, the evaluation of the desirability of load shedding local government services to RCAs is far more complicated than determining if RCAs can provide certain services more efficiently and effectively than local governments. That evaluation is also affected by one's view concerning two of the most fundamental and controversial questions of governance: what is the appropriate role of the public sector in regulating economic activity and where should the locus of economic and political power reside, at the national, state, local, or neighborhood levels.

RCAs' Impact on Local Government Politics and Elections

The 1990 nationwide survey of RCA board members indicated that RCA board members regularly monitor the actions of local government officials and will not hesitate to let them know their views when police protection is perceived to be wanting, or when local development, traffic patterns, or zoning decisions are perceived to jeopardize their neighborhood's quality of life or property values. The results of Barton and Silverman's 1986 survey of RCA board presidents in California and ACIR's 1988 nationwide survey of RCA board members confirm that RCA board members and officers are active participants in the NIMBY movement. However, the California and ACIR surveys also indicated that relatively few RCAs have ongoing committees dedicated to studying or acting upon general governmental issues. Believing that positions on such issues are the prerogative of the individual voter and fearing the divisive effect of conflict over such issues on their own relationships within the association, RCAs rarely endorse political candidates or take public positions on issues that do not directly affect the neighborhood's property values or perceived quality of life. For example, the 1990 survey revealed that only 4 percent of the respondent's RCAs had ever endorsed a political candidate (Dilger 1990). While some associations do invite elected officials and candidates to speak with members of the board of directors or to the association's membership at a community forum, the most prevailing attitude among RCA board members concerning their local government officials is "if you leave us alone, we'll leave you alone" (Barton and Silverman 1988; Dean 1989; Community Associations Institute 1989).

The implications of RCAs' lobbying efforts have not been fully explored and represent a major new area for scholarly attention. RCAs may serve as the primary vehicle for promoting participation in local political affairs in areas where party organizations are weak. They may also serve as important alternative vehicles for promoting political participation in areas where party organizations are strong. However, RCAs' lobbying efforts are primarily focused on issues that impact their neighborhood directly, such as zoning, traffic patterns, and development. As a result, their role as facilitators of local political participation is muted and is likely to be a significant factor only on a case-by-case basis.

RCAs may also serve as important new incubators for political organizers and, to a lesser extent, for local political candidates as well (Kleine 1989). RCA board members know their neighborhoods and have ready access to names and telephone numbers. They are also among the opinion leaders in their neighborhood. As a result, local political candidates are increasingly turning to RCA leaders to serve as precinct captains and head neighborhood get-out-the vote efforts. Moreover, there is anecdotal evidence that increasing numbers of RCA board members are either considering or have actually run for local political office. In addition, 5 percent of the respondents to the 1990 nationwide survey of RCA board members indicated that they were more likely to run for political office as a result of their experiences with their RCA.

RCAs' lobbying efforts have not only affected the decisions reached by local government officials but are also beginning to alter the agenda of issues that are discussed at the local government level. For example, local government officials are increasingly facing demands from RCA members for tax reimbursements and for a greater voice in determining neighborhood zoning decisions. Moreover, RCAs are also beginning to lobby their state legislatures. RCA members in New Jersey, for example, recently embarked on an extensive letter writing campaign that resulted in their state government enacting the nation's first statewide legislation mandating local government reimbursement to RCAs for the provision of public services. In this case, the state law mandates RCA reimbursement for snow and ice removal, street lighting, and collection of leaves, recyclables, and garbage (Krugh 1990). Similar letter writing campaigns are expected to be launched throughout the nation over the next several years.

RCAs' Impact on Political Socialization and Civic Virtue

RCAs advocates applaud the emergence of RCAs as an opportunity for people of similar backgrounds and values to join together to create a strong sense of community at the local level. They suggest that in contrast to government, which is often remote and bureaucratic, RCAs provide an opportunity for direct democracy where neighbors meet face to face to resolve their common problems. This interaction, they argue, promotes a stronger sense of civic virtue because neighbors recognize the efficacy of their participation in RCA meetings.

The evidence concerning RCA's impact on civic virtue is mixed (see Chapter 7). It can be argued, on a case-by-case basis, that RCAs do heighten community awareness of some local political issues, that they do provide a political base for some to enter political life, and that they do provide, through regular neighborhood meetings, an additional arena for political interaction. However, many RCA members react to the internal politics of RCAs in the same manner in which they react to governmental politics: they do not participate. As mentioned previously, many RCAs experience a very difficult time achieving a quorum at their general membership meetings, many RCAs have a difficult time filling all of the vacancies on their board of directors, and many RCAs are unable to get enough people to volunteer to fill all of the vacancies on their committees and task forces (Barton and Silverman 1987a, 1989; Dale and McBee 1988; Brooks 1990a). This suggests that many RCA members are free riders, relying on others to do all the organizational work while they enjoy the collective benefits that this work produces. As a result, the ability of RCAs to promote civic virtue and impact the political socialization of its members is muted because many RCA members will participate in their RCA's affairs only when they feel that their interests are being threatened by its decisions or when they perceive that they need their RCA's assistance in defending their property values and quality of life.

Should RCAs Be Regulated?

Given the inevitability of RCAs in the United States, their growing impact on local government and politics, and the important role they play in determining how Americans interact both with government and with others in their neighborhood, it is prudent to determine what constitutes a successful RCA and what actions are appropriate to ensure that RCAs have an opportunity to be successful. However, just as beauty is in the eye of the beholder, the definition of a successful RCA is largely determined by one's values and perspective. For example, when attorneys evaluate RCAs they tend to focus on the legal implications that arise when RCAs enforce the neighborhood's CC&Rs (servitudes). In their view, when an individual purchases a home in a RCA-governed neighborhood and voluntarily subjects themselves to its CC&Rs they are actually entering into a contract with the other members of the RCA. Typically, it is assumed that individuals freely and knowingly relinquish some of their private property rights to the group in the expectation that the CC&Rs will enhance their property values and quality of life. However, the courts have determined that contracts are enforceable only if all parties to the contract are given an opportunity to fully understand the contract's provisions and its implications. As a result, most attorneys are convinced that government has both the right and the obligation to issue regulations that require all sellers to fully disclose all RCA-related documents to purchasers prior to the closing on a home subject to RCA governance. In addition, the courts have determined that contracts are enforceable because they provide important benefits to all the parties involved. RCAs' primary benefits include protection of the neighborhood's property values and the enhancement of individual choice by allowing individuals an opportunity to create a living environment that they believe will maximize their self-fulfillment. However, some attorneys have argued that some of the servitudes used by RCAs are not enforceable by the courts because they obstruct other, more important societal goals, such as the efficient utilization of land, democratic participation in local land-use decisions, or the protection of personal autonomy and identity. They argue that government has a right and an obligation to issue regulations to prevent RCAs from obstructing these more important goals. They are also convinced that government regulations are a more efficient way to promote these goals than to rely on the courts' rulings on litigation. Specifically, they want government to require RCAs to restrict the duration of servitudes to no longer than twenty years and to allow RCA members to terminate and modify existing CC&Rs by a two-thirds vote instead of by the more widely used unanimous consent rule (Winokur 1989b, 1990; Korngold 1990).

Real estate developers and local government officials have a slightly different focus than attorneys. Real estate developers tend to evaluate RCAs in terms of their impact on their local housing market, their profits, and the likelihood of securing building permits from their local government. As a result, they do not have a preconceived notion of what constitutes a successful RCA. In their view, home buyers will determine what constitutes a successful RCA. If home buyers in their area determine that a successful RCA is one that offers X number and type of services and Y number and type of covenants, then the real estate industry will propose RCAs that provide X number and type of services and Y number and type of covenants. If home buyers in their area want RCAs that adhere to the one person, one vote governance model, the real estate industry will propose RCAs that adhere to that governance model. As a result, those involved in the real estate industry tend to oppose government regulation of RCAs. In their view, the market is better able to determine what constitutes a successful RCA than government officials. Moreover, since each local housing market is unique, the definition of what constitutes a successful RCA will vary from area to area, making it extremely difficult for local or state government officials to create regulations that will fit the desires of consumers in as precise a manner as will the local housing market.

Local government officials tend to measure the success or failure of RCAs in terms of their management functions. If the RCA is managing its financial resources well, local government officials can focus their financial resources and attention in other areas of their community. Although many RCAs formed during the 1970s and early 1980s may soon experience financial difficulties as their infrastructure ages, relatively few RCAs have approached local government officials for financial assistance and even fewer have ever gone bankrupt. This may help to explain why local governments generally do not regulate RCAs' internal operating procedures and fiscal behavior. Their prevailing attitude seems to be: why attempt to fix something that is not broken. One RCA advocate has even gone so far as to suggest that it is amazing that in the absence of any significant support or assistance from national, state, or local government entities that RCAs are surviving at all (Dowden 1980).

When RCA members evaluate their RCAs they primarily focus on management functions, specifically how efficiently and effectively they provide services, enforce the neighborhood's CC&Rs, and enhance the neighborhood's aesthetics and, subsequently, property values. Surveys also suggest that they are interested in having an opportunity to participate in its decisions. Although they may choose not to participate on a regular basis, as long as they know that they have an opportunity to have their voice heard and are confident that the RCA's board of directors and officers are fair, impartial, and reasonable most of them will be satisfied that the RCA's actions are legitimate (Norcross 1973; Dowden 1980).

There has been very little research on the attitudes of RCA members toward government regulation of RCA internal operating procedures and fiscal behavior. For example, it is not known what percentage of RCA members want government to require RCAs to complete reserve studies, to provide them an opportunity to terminate and modify CC&Rs by a two-thirds vote as opposed to unanimous consent, to mandate that the CC&Rs automatically expire at the end of a set period of time, or to base voting rights on the one person, one vote principle. However, the 1990 survey did ask RCA board members to answer the following open-ended question: If you were suddenly given the power to make one change in the way local governments affect community associations, what one change would you make? The responses to this open-ended question varied widely, but one pattern did emerge. RCA board members want more formal mechanisms in place to facilitate communication between local government officials and RCAs (Dilger 1990).

The relatively few social scientists that have examined RCAs offer yet another unique perspective concerning RCAs. Most social scientists share a paradigm of what constitutes a fair and equitable political system. That paradigm is based on the pluralistic model, where interest groups are at the heart of politics and policymaking and play an important role in producing policies that are responsive to public desires (Cigler and Loomis 1986). In their view, group activity is a desirable way for individuals to exert influence on the policymaking process. They also assume as axiomatic that there is ordinarily no clearly defined and agreed upon conception of what constitutes the public interest on most issues. Instead, the public interest emerges from the contention of a multiplicity of self-interested actors, with the group struggle for power serving as an adversarial process that produces a degree of rationality that otherwise would not exist in the policymaking process. However, for this adversarial process to occur and work properly, all groups with a stake in the issue at hand must be represented and group leaders must faithfully represent the collective interests of their memberships (Hayes 1986).

As a result of their paradigm, social scientists tend to pay greater attention to RCA's internal operating procedures than do attorney's, real estate developers, and local government officials because they are interested in the way RCAs represent the interests of its members to other groups and institutions in American society. In their view, the pluralistic model requires that RCAs' internal decisionmaking processes operate in a way that ensures that the actions taken by RCA board members are representative of its members' desires. Otherwise, those actions cannot be considered as legitimate inputs into the political system. As a result, social scientists tend to advocate government regulations that will ensure that all RCA members and residents subject to RCA governance have an opportunity to participate in its meetings, influence its decisions, and keep its leaders accountable to their desires. To accomplish these goals, government should require RCAs to provide its members with prior notification of all general membership and board of directors meetings, prohibit closed meetings that exclude any member of the association or any affected individuals from having an opportunity to ask questions, make comments and offer suggestions, base RCA suffrage rights on the one person, one vote principle, or, alternatively, provide mechanisms to ensure that renters are not disenfranchised, and mandate the completion and dissemination of reserve studies and other appropriate documents (such as the RCA's CC&Rs and bylaws) to all members of the RCA as well as to those considering the purchase of a home in the RCA.

Some Concluding Remarks

Overall, RCAs generally meet the expectations of RCA members, real estate developers, and local government officials. That is why consumers continue to purchase homes in PUD and condominium developments, why real estate developers continue to propose PUD and condominium developments, and why local governments continue to approve most of those proposals. However, local governments have a substantial economic stake in the success of RCAs. RCAs not only subsidize infrastructure and service delivery expenses that would ordinarily burden local government but through the enforcement of their CC&Rs they also augment local government's property tax revenue. As a result, local governments have an economic interest in developing a strategy that fosters and supports the operation of RCAs that have the capacity, viability, and resources to carry out their responsibilities (Dowden 1980).

Specifically, local governments should protect their interests by developing a capacity to keep informed of the ongoing operations of RCAs within their jurisdictions and implement programs to provide them with technical assistance and financial advice. All too often, many local governments discover that a problem exists with one of their RCAs only after the problem has escalated to the stage of confrontation and dissension. The 1990 survey results indicated that RCA board members recognize that this problem exists and want more formal mechanisms in place to facilitate communication between themselves and local government officials (Dilger 1990). Some analysts, particularly those connected with the real estate industry, have suggested that government monitoring of RCA activities and the offering of management advice may be beneficial for all parties concerned, particularly for many of the smaller RCAs across the United States that are not members of the Community Associations Institute and do not have access to their publications, seminars, and workshops. However, they are not convinced that government should impose mandatory regulations on RCA activities and internal operating procedures. If there are any serious problems, they believe that the economic law of supply and demand will find the solution. For example, when the dissatisfaction with the transition from developer to homeowner control began to affect the demand for condominiums during the 1960s and 1970s (see Chapter 3), the real estate industry, in cooperation with the Community Associations Institute, reevaluated its behavior and fixed the problem areas, particularly concerning the establishment of initial assessment fees by developers that were unrealistically low.

Although the real estate industry deserves commendation for making adjustments over the years to correct obvious problems, its perspective is too narrow. It fails to recognize that government has an obligation to enforce and regulate contracts. The legal profession is correct when it argues that each RCA's CC&Rs is a binding contract among individuals seeking to maximize their economic self-interests through collective action. As a result, government has both the right and an obligation to ensure that all RCA documents are disclosed to anyone contemplating the purchase of a home in a RCA-governed neighborhood because all parties to a contract must be given an opportunity to fully understand the contract's provisions and its implications. Otherwise, the contract will not be considered enforceable by the courts. However, even the legal profession's prevailing view of RCAs as economic contracts is too narrow. RCAs represent much more than just an economic contract among individuals seeking to maximize their economic self-interests through collective action. Although RCAs' activities have economic value for their members, their CC&Rs also create boundaries for social interaction and behavior that are designed to shape and maximize the neighborhood's social living environment. The contract implicit in the neighborhood's CC&Rs is similar to the social contract that underlies the constitutional relationship that exists between individuals and government. As a result, RCAs are much more than just nonprofit corporations. They are private governments by contract.

Since RCAs are private governments, the same principles that apply to government's internal operating procedures should also apply to RCAs. Specifically, government should require RCAs to provide its members with prior notification of all general membership and board of directors meetings, prohibit closed meetings that exclude any member of the association or any affected individuals from having an opportunity to ask questions, make comments, and offer suggestions, base RCA suffrage rights on the one person, one vote principle or, alternatively, provide mechanisms to ensure that renters are not disenfranchised, and mandate the completion and dissemination of reserve studies and other appropriate documents (such as the RCA's CC&Rs and bylaws) to all members of the RCA as well as to those considering the purchase of a home in the RCA. Otherwise, the ability of RCA members to hold their elected leaders accountable for their actions will be compromised and the likelihood that the actions of the RCA's board of directors will fail to be representative of the desires of its general membership will be increased. If either of these events takes place, the social contract that serves as the foundation for the formation of the association will be violated. Social contracts are based on the assumption that each individual has an equal opportunity to participate in the collective decisions that affect him or her and that those decisions will be representative of the members' wishes. Otherwise, no one would agree voluntarily to join the association or to subject themselves to its collective authority.

Although contractual obligations are important, it is inappropriate to use them as the only basis for determining if, and how, government should regulate RCAs' activities and internal operating procedures. That decision should also take into consideration RCAs' impact on the distribution of power within society as a whole. Some critics maintain that RCAs are not desirable because they represent yet another mechanism for the relatively affluent to influence the outcome of public policy. According to this view, RCAs are primarily composed of middle to upper income families. Middle to upper income families tend to have greater access to and influence with state and local government decisionmakers than those who are economically disadvantaged. Thus, RCAs' lobbying efforts exacerbate the power differential that currently exists among economic classes in the United States. To promote a more equitable society, RCAs' critics argue that government should use its regulatory powers to curtail existing RCAs' lobbying activities and its zoning and planning powers to prevent the formation of additional RCAs. Similarly, some critics have suggested that government should use its regulatory powers to limit the extent of RCAs' lobbying efforts and its zoning and planning powers to prevent the formation of additional RCAs because they represent yet another political obstacle that must be hurdled by government officials who wish to make policy decisions that reflect the interests of the entire community as opposed to the interests of particular neighborhoods.

However, these arguments erroneously assume that there is a direct, causal relationship between the inputs to the political system and its outputs. They neglect the important role policymakers play in the policymaking process. Ideally, policymakers consider the input of all interested parties, using that input to help them reach decisions that are in the public's interest. Of course, there is a socioeconomic skew toward the more highly educated and wealthy for all forms of political activity, including voting, campaigning, and lobbying. The interests of the poor are often not fully represented in the American political system (Schlozman and Tierney

1986). However, RCAs should not be held accountable for this deficiency. Although the interests of certain segments of the population, particularly the poor, are ordinarily not fully represented, understood, or appreciated, RCAs should be applauded for providing individuals with an additional opportunity to provide responsible input into the American political system. Policymakers do not always receive input from all interested parties when making their decisions and, as a result, are often denied an opportunity to be enlightened by the presentation of disparate points of view. However, RCAs' lobbying efforts move us closer to that pluralistic ideal and augment the prospects of responsible policymakers reaching decisions that are in the public interest.

References

Advisory Commission on Intergovernmental Relations (ACIR). 1978. *Categorical Grants: Their Role and Design.* Washington, DC: U.S. Government Printing Office.

———. 1980. *Citizen Participation in the American Federal System.* Washington, DC: U.S. Government Printing Office.

———. 1981. *The Condition of Contemporary Federalism.* Washington, DC: ACIR.

———. 1985. *The Question of State Government Capability.* Washington, DC: ACIR.

———. 1988. Two Worlds of Local Government: Residential Community Associations in the Intergovernmental System. Staff report. Washington, DC: ACIR.

———. 1989. *Residential Community Associations: Private Governments in the Intergovernmental System?* Washington, DC: ACIR.

———. 1990. *Significant Features of Fiscal Federalism: Volume 1, Budget Processes and Tax Systems.* Washington, DC: ACIR.

Aranson, Peter H. 1990. Federalism: The Reasons of Rules. *the Cato Journal* 10:1 (Spring/Summer): 17–38.

Armoa, Jo-Ann. 1989. A $335,000 Good-Neighbor Gesture. *The Washington Post,* June 22: D3.

Associations and the IRS. 1988. 8th. Edition. Alexandria, VA: Communities Association Institute.

Bair, Lowell. ed. 1974. *The Essential Rousseau.* New York: New American Library.

Barfield, Claude E. 1981. *Rethinking Federalism.* Washington, DC: American Enterprise Institute for Public Policy.

Barton, Stephen E. and Carol Silverman. 1987. *Common Interest Homeowners' Associations Management Study.* Sacramento, CA: California Department of Real Estate.

———. 1987. Overcoming Conflicts and Frustration in Running a Community Association. *Common Ground* (September/October): 12–15, 25–27.

———. 1988. Common Interest Homeowners' Associations: Private Government and The Public Interest Revisited. *Public Affairs Report* (May): 5–9.

———. 1989. The Political Life of Mandatory Homeowners' Associations. In *Residential Community Associations: Private Governments in the Intergovernmental System?* Pp. 31–37. See ACIR.

Beam, David R. 1978. Why Categorical Grants? In *Categorical Grants: Their Role and Design.* ed. David Walker. Pp. 49–59. Washington, DC: U.S. Government Printing Office.

Beam, David R.; Timothy J. Conlan and David B. Walker. 1983. Federalism: The Challenge of Conflicting Theories and Contemporary Practice. In *Political Science: The State of the Discipline.* ed. Ada W. Finifter. Pp. 247–279. Washington, DC: American Political Science Association.

Beer, Samuel. 1974. The Modernization of American Federalism. In *The Federal Polity.* ed. Daniel J. Elazar. Pp. 49–95. New Brunswick, NJ: Transaction Books.

Bendick, Marc Jr. 1984. Privatization of Public Services: Recent Experiences. In *Public-Private Partnership: New Opportunities for Meeting Social Needs.* eds. Harvey Brooks, Lance Liebman, and Corrine S. Schelling. Cambridge, MA: Ballinger.

Bennett, James T. and Thomas J. Dilorenzo. 1987. The Role of Tax-Funded Politics. *Proceedings of the Academy of Political Science* 36:3 (Spring): 14–23.

Beyle, Thad L. 1988. The Governor as Innovator in the Federal System. *Publius* 18 (Summer): 131–152.

Bowman, Ann O'M. and Kearney, Richard C. 1986. *The Resurgence of the States.* Englewood Cliffs, NJ: Prentice-Hall.

Brasfield, James M. 1989. Reorganizing St. Louis County: The Debate Goes On. *Intergovernmental Perspective* (Winter): 24–27.

Brooks, Andree. 1990a. Putting Together A Quorum. *New York Times.* April 22: R9, R14.

———. 1990b. Adhering To Tough New Rules. *New York Times.* May 20: R9, R16.

———. 1990c. Securing Municipal Rights. *New York Times.* July 9: R3, R10.

———. 1990d. Confusion And Relief On Taxes. *New York Times.* July 30: R5, R8.

Burns, James MacGregor; J. W. Peltason; and Thomas E. Cronin. 1990. *Government By The People.* 14th ed. Englewood Cliffs, NJ: Prentice-Hall.

Cahn, Joseph M. 1987. Developer v. Condo Association. *Real Estate Today* (April): 58, 59.

CAI News. 1989. Local Issues: How Far Should Associations Go? *CAI News,* Vol. XIV, No. 10: 2.

CAI Research Foundation. 1987. Survey on Association Communications. *Common Ground* (September/October): 7.

Campbell-Bell, D.K. 1985. Homeowners Associations—Is Tax Exemption Worth the Effort? *Real Property Probate and Trust Journal* 20 (Summer): 647–662.

Cigler, Allan J. and Burdett A. Loomis. 1986. Editors. *Interest Group Politics.* 2nd. ed. Washington, DC: Congressional Quarterly.

Clark, Peter B. and James Q. Wilson. 1961. Incentive Systems: A Theory of Organizations. *Administrative Science Quarterly.* 6 (September): 129–166.

Clurman, David, Scott F. Jackson and Edna Hebard. 1984. *Condominiums and Cooperatives,* Second Edition. New York: John Wiley & Sons.

Colella, Cynthia Cates. 1981. Breakdown of Constitutional Constraints: Interpretive Variations From The First Constitutional Revolution To The Fourth. In *The Condition of Contemporary Federalism: Conflicting Theories and Collapsing Constraints.* ed. David B. Walker. Pp. 27–110. Washington, DC: U.S. Government Printing Office.

———. 1986. The United States Supreme Court and Intergovernmental Relations. In *American Intergovernmental Relations Today: Perspectives and Controversies.* ed. Robert J. Dilger. Englewood Cliffs, NJ: Prentice-Hall.

Community Associations Institute. 1988. *Community Associations Factbook.* Alexandria, VA: Community Associations Institute.

———. 1989. Community Associations and Public Officials: A Roundtable Discussion. *Common Ground* 5 (May/June): 18–21.

Conlan, Timothy. 1981. Alternative Perspectives on Federalism. In *The Condition of Contemporary Federalism: Conflicting Theories and Collapsing Constraints.* ed. David B. Walker. Pp. 1–25. Washington, DC: U.S. Government Printing Office.

———. 1981b. Government Unlocked: Political Constraints on Federal Growth Since The 1930s. In *The Condition of Contemporary Federalism: Conflicting Theories and Collapsing Constraints.* ed. David B. Walker. Pp. 111–140. Washington, DC: U.S. Government Printing Office.

———. 1986. Federalism and Competing Values in the Reagan Administration. *Publius* 16 (Winter): 29–47.

———. 1988. *New Federalism: Intergovernmental Reform From Nixon to Reagan.* Washington, DC: The Brookings Institution.

Conlan, Timothy and David Walker. 1983. Reagan's New Federalism: Design, Debate, and Discord. *Intergovernmental Perspective* 18:4 (Winter): 6–22.

Cowan, Martin B. 1978. Tax Reform on the Home Front: Cooperative

Housing Corporations, Condominiums, and Homeowners Associations. *Journal of Real Estate Taxation* (Winter): 101–141.

Dale, John G. and Kim McBee. 1988. Voluntary Involvement Survey. *Common Ground* (May/June): 9, 11, 33.

De Alessi, Louis. 1987. Property Rights and Privatization. *Proceedings of the Academy of Political Science* 36:3 (Spring): 25–35.

Dean, Debra L. 1988. Two Worlds of Local Government: Residential Community Associations in the Intergovernmental System. Staff report. Washington, DC: ACIR.

———. 1989. Community Association and Local Government Relationships: Attitudes and Services. *Common Ground* 5 (May/June): 24–26.

Diamond, Martin. 1974. The Ends of Federalism. In *The Federal Polity*. ed. Daniel J. Elazar. Pp. 129–152. New Brunswick, NJ: Transaction Books.

———. 1985. What the Framers Meant By Federalism. In *American Intergovernmental Relations*. ed. Laurence J. O'Toole, Jr. Pp. 28–35. Washington, DC: Congressional Quarterly Press.

Diaz, Raymond. 1988. The Fiduciary Duty of the Association Manager. *Common Ground* (May/June): 13–17.

Dilger, Robert J. 1986. The Expansion and Centralization of American Governmental Functions. In *American Intergovernmental Relations Today: Perspectives and Controversies*. ed. Robert J. Dilger. Pp. 5–29. Englewood Cliffs, NJ: Prentice-Hall.

———. 1989. *National Intergovernmental Programs*. Englewood Cliffs, NJ: Prentice-Hall.

———. 1990. Nationwide survey of CAI-member RCAs. Results available from the author. Morgantown, WV: Institute for Public Affairs, West Virginia University.

———. 1991. Residential Community Associations: Issues, Impacts, and Relevance for Local Government. *State and Local Government Review* (Winter): 17–23.

Dowden, C. James. 1980. *Community Associations: A Guide for Public Officials*. Washington, DC: The Urban Land Institute.

———. 1986. *Creating A Community Association: The Developer's Role in Condominium and Homeowner Associations*. 2d rev. ed. Washington, DC: Urban Land Institute.

———. 1989. Community Associations and Local Governments: The Need for Recognition and Reassessment. In *Residential Community Associations: Private Governments in the Intergovernmental System?* Pp. 27–30. See ACIR.

Elazar, Daniel. 1968. Federalism. In *International Encyclopedia of the Social Sciences*. Vol. 5. Ed. David Sills. New York: MacMillan Co. and Free Press. Cited in Timothy Conlan. 1981. Government Unlocked: Political Constraints on Federal Growth Since The 1930s. In *The Condition of Contemporary Federalism: Conflicting Theories and Collapsing*

Constraints. ed. David B. Walker. Pp. 111–140. Washington, DC: U.S. Government Printing Office.

———. 1974. The New Federalism: Can the States Be Trusted? *Public Interest* 35 (Spring): 89–102.

Ellickson, Robert C. 1982. Cities and Homeowners Associations. *University of Pennsylvania Law Review:* 1519–1580.

———. 1982. A Reply to Michelman and Frug. *University of Pennsylvania Law Review:* 1602–1608.

Elliot, Donald. 1989. Reconciling Perspectives on the St. Louis Metropolitan Area. *Intergovernmental Perspective* (Winter): 17–19.

Fairfield, Roy P. 1966. Editor. *The Federalist Papers*. 2nd ed. Garden City, NY: Anchor Books.

Federal Housing Administration. 1965. *Suggested Legal Documents for Planned-Unit Developments*. Washington, DC: U.S. Government Printing Office.

Fixler, Philip E. Jr., and Robert W. Poole, Jr. 1987. *Proceedings of The Academy of Political Science* 36:3 (Spring): 164–189.

Frank, Barry H. 1976. IRS takes harsh position on exempting condominium and homeowners' associations. *Real Estate* (May 1976): 306–310.

Frazier, Mark. 1984. *Stimulating Community Enterprise: A Response to Fiscal Strains in the Public Sector,* Joint Economic Committee, U.S. Congress; Joint Committee Print, S. 98–276. Washington, DC: U.S. Government Printing Office.

———. 1989. Seeding Grass Roots Recovery: New Catalysts for Community Associations. In *Residential Community Associations:Private Governments in the Intergovernmental* System? Pp. 63–68. See ACIR.

Friedman, Milton. 1962. *Capitalism, Freedom and Democracy*. Chicago: Chicago University Press.

Friedman, Milton and Rose Friedman. 1979. *Free to Choose*. New York: Harcourt Brace Jovanovich.

Frug, Gerald E. 1980. The City as a Legal Concept. *Harvard Law Review:* 1059–1151.

———. 1982. Cities and Homeowners Associations: A Reply. *University of Pennsylvania Law Review:* 1589–1601.

Gans, Curtis B. 1989. The Problem of Nonvoting. In *Points of View*. 4th ed. Eds. Robert E. DiClerico and Allan S. Hammock. Pp. 91–99. New York: Random House.

Garreau, Joel. 1987. The Shadow Governments. *The Washington Post,* June 14: A1, A14.

Gordon, Robert J. 1984. *Macroeconomics*. Third ed. Boston: Little, Brown and Company.

Hartz, Louis. 1955. *The Liberal Tradition in America*. New York: Harcourt, Brace & World, Inc.

Harwood, Richard. 1980. Americans-1980. In *The Pursuit of the Presidency 1980*. ed. Richard Harwood. Pp. 3–18. New York: Berkley Books.

Hawkins, Robert B. 1989. Preface to *Residential Community Associations: Private Governments in the Intergovernmental System?* See ACIR 1989.

Hayes, Michael T. 1986. The New Group Universe. In *Interest Group Politics.* 2nd. ed. Edited by Allan J. Cigler and Burdett A. Loomis. Pp. 133–145. Washington, DC: Congressional Quarterly.

Heffner, Richard D. 1956. Editor. *Democracy in America* by Alexis de Tocqueville. New York: New American Library.

Henig, Jeffrey R. 1985. *Public Policy and Federalism: Issues in State and Local Politics.* New York: St. Martin's Press.

———. 1990. Privatization in the United States. *Political Science Quarterly* 104:4: 649–670.

Hickok, Eugene W., Jr. 1990. Federalism's Future before the U.S. Supreme Court. *The Annals* 509 (May): 73–82.

Holland, Charlotte. 1989. Focus for second high school now on two locations. *Redlands Daily Facts,* January 17: A1, A3.

Homeowner Board Service Provides Broad Education. 1984. *Los Angeles Times,* March 25: E2.

Hornblower, Margaret. 1988. Not in My Backyard, You Don't. *Time,* June 27: 44, 45.

Howard, A.E. Dick. 1986. *Garcia:* Of Federalism and Constitutional Values. *Publius* 16 (Summer): 18–31.

Hunter, Lawrence A. and Ronald J. Oakerson. 1986. An Intellectual Crisis in American Federalism: The Meaning of *Garcia. Publius* 16 (Summer): 33–50.

Hyatt, Wayne S. 1985. *Condominiums and Homeowner Associations: A Guide to the Development Process.* New York: McGraw Hill.

———. 1988. *Condominium and Homeowner Association Practice: Community Association Law.* 2nd. ed. Philadelphia: American Law Institute.

Hyatt, Wayne S., and Philip S. Downer. 1987. *Condominium and Homeowner Association Litigation: Community Association Law.* NY: John Wiley & Sons.

Isaacson, Andrew L. and Earl L. Segal. 1981. Community Associations: The Common Tread. *Real Estate Review* 11 (Spring): 84–90.

Jackson, F. Scott. 1977. A Developer's Guide to Homeowners' Associations. *Real Estate Review* 7 (Fall): 79–85.

———. 1978. How Homeowners Associations Solve Their Enforcement Problems. *Real Estate Review* 8 (Spring): 80–86.

Jackson, F. Scott and David G. Baratti. 1982. *Strategies for Successful Enforcement of Rules and Deed Restrictions.* Alexandria, VA: Communities Association Institute.

Judd, Dennis R. 1988. *The Politics of American Cities.* 3rd. Ed. Glenview, IL: Scott, Foresman and Company.

Katz, Jeffrey L. 1990. Neighborhood Politics: A Changing World. *Governing* (November): 48–54.

———. 1991. Privatizing without Tears. *Governing* (June): 38–42.

Kennedy, David M. 1987. Federalism and the Force of History. In *How Federal Is The Constitution?* ed. Robert A. Goldwin and William A. Schambra. Pp. 67–83. Washington, DC: American Enterprise Institute for Public Policy Research.

Kettl, Donald F. 1979. Can the Cities Be Trusted: The Community Development Experience. *Political Science Quarterly* (Fall): 437–451.

Klein, Dianne. 1988. The Power of Homeowner Associations. *Los Angeles Times,* October 28: 1, 36.

Kleine, Douglas. 1989. Director of Research, Community Associations Institute. Interview by author, June 22. Alexandria, VA.

Korngold, Gerald. 1990. Resolving the Flaws of Residential Servitudes and Owners Associations: For Reformation Not Termination. *Wisconsin Law Review* 2: 513–535.

Krugh, Robert C. 1990. President, Community Associations Institute, New Jersey Chapter. Letter concerning New Jersey's Community Association Laws. February 6.

Leach, Richard. 1970. *American Federalism.* New York: W.W. Norton.

Longhini, Gregory, and David Mosena. 1978. *Homeowners' Associations: Problems and Remedies.* Chicago, IL: American Planning Association.

Loomis, Burdett A. and Allan J. Cigler. 1986. Introduction: The Changing Nature of Interest Group Politics. In *Interest Group Politics.* 2nd. ed. Eds. Allan J. Cigler and Burdett A. Loomis. Pp. 1–26. Washington, DC: Congressional Quarterly, Inc.

Louv, Richard. 1983. But Can We Fight the New Tyranny of Our Neighbors? *The Washington Post,* November 6: D1, D2.

Managing a Successful Community Association. 1974. Washington, DC: the Urban Land Institute.

Mansbridge, Jane J. 1980. *Beyond Adversary Democracy.* New York: Basic Books.

Marchese, John. 1987. What a Revoltin' Development This Is. *Philadelphia Magazine,* (May): 125–128, 179–184.

McConnell. 1984. *Economics.* 9th ed. New York: McGraw-Hill.

McDowell, Gary L. 1987. Federalism and Civic Virtue: The Antifederalists and the Constitution. In *How Federal is the Constitution?* eds. Robert A. Goldwin and William A. Schambra. Pp. 122–144. Washington, DC: American Enterprise Institute for Public Policy.

Metropolitan Washington Council of Governments. 1976. *Condominium Housing: A New Homeownership Alternative for Metropolitan Washington.* Washington, DC: Metropolitan Washington Council of Governments.

Meyer, Ralph C. 1988. Democracy or Dictatorship: Are Association Leaders Listening? *Common Ground* (May/June): 18–21.

Miller, Dean J. 1989. Life Cycle of an RCA. In *Residential Community*

Associations: Private Governments in the Intergovernmental System? Pp. 39–44. See ACIR.

Miller, James P. 1990. Condo Warfare. *Wall Street Journal,* May 19: R26.

Montesquieu. 1961. extracts from *The Spirit of the Laws, Book VIII.* In *The Great Political Theories.* ed. Michael Curtis. Pp. 395–396. New York: Avon Books. Cited in Conlan, Timothy. 1981. Alternative Perspectives on Federalism. In *The Condition of Contemporary Federalism: Conflicting Theories and Collapsing Constraints.* ed. David B. Walker. Pp. 6. Washington, DC: U.S. Government Printing Office.

Moore, Stephen. 1987. Contracting Out: A Painless Alternative to the Budget Cutter's Knife. *Proceedings of the Academy of Political Science* 36:3 (Spring): 61–73.

Murphy, Kim. 1986. $100 Million Asked in Suit Against Solar Contractors. *The Los Angeles Times,* July 22: 3, 15.

Nelson, Robert H. 1989. The Privatization of Local Government: From Zoning to RCAs. In *Residential Community Associations: Private Governments in the Intergovernmental System?* Pp. 45–52. See ACIR.

Norcross, Carl. 1973. *Townhouses and Condominiums: Residents' Likes and Dislikes.* Washington, DC: The Urban Land Institute.

Oakerson, Ronald J. 1989a. Private Street Associations in St. Louis County: Subdivisions as Service Providers. In *Residential Community Associations: Private Governments in the Intergovernmental System?* Pp. 55–61. See ACIR.

———. 1989b. Residential Community Associations: Further Differentiating the Organization of Local Public Economies. In *Residential Community Associations: Private Governments in the Intergovernmental System?* Pp. 105–110. See ACIR.

Oates, Wallace. 1972. *Fiscal Federalism.* New York: Harcourt, Brace, Jovanovich.

Olson, Mancur. 1965. *The Logic of Collective Action.* Cambridge, MA: Harvard University Press.

Parker, Rosetta E. 1984. *Housing for the Elderly: The Handbook for Managers.* Alexandria, VA: Communities Association Institute.

Parks, Roger B. and Ronald J. Oakerson. 1989. St. Louis: The ACIR Study. *Intergovernmental Perspective* (Winter): 9–11.

Peterson, Iver. 1990. When a Man's Condo Is Not His Castle. *New York Times,* February 11: R1, R12.

Phares, Donald. 1989. Reorganizing The St. Louis Area: The Freeholders' Plan. *Intergovernmental Perspective* (Winter): 12–16.

Pierson, John. 1989. The Decline and Fall of Town Meetings. In *State and Local Government.* 4th ed. ed. Bruce Stinebrickner. Pp. 87–89. Guilford, CT: Dushkin Publishers.

Polsby, Nelson W. 1989. Prospects for Pluralism. In *Readings in American Government and Politics.* eds. Randall B. Ripley and Elliot E. Slotnick. Pp. 131–137. New York: McGraw-Hill Book Company.

Ranney. Austin. 1989. Nonvoting Is Not a Social Disease. In *Points of View*. 4th ed. Eds. Robert E. DiClerico and Allan S. Hammock. Pp. 91–99. New York: Random House.

Reeves, Mavis Mann. 1990. The States as Polities: Reformed, Reinvigorated, Resourceful. *Annals* 509 (May): 83–93.

Rosenberry, Katharine. 1985. Actions of Community Association Boards: When Are They Valid and When Do They Create Liability? *Real Estate Law Journal* 13 (Spring): 315–333.

———. 1989. Condominium and Homeowner Associations: Should They Be Treated Like "Mini-Governments?" In *Residential Community Associations: Private Governments in the Intergovernmental System?* Pp. 69–74. See ACIR.

Salamon, Lester. 1989. The Changing Tools of Government Action. In *Beyond Privatization: The Tools of Government Action.* Washington, DC: Urban Institute Press.

Salisbury, Robert H. 1969. An Exchange Theory of Interest Groups. *Midwest Journal of Political Science* 13:1 (February): 1–32.

Savas, E.S. 1987. *Privatization: The Key to Better Government.* Chatham, NJ: Chatham House Publishers.

Scannell, Nancy. 1986. Courtlands Neighbors Complete Package Deal. *The Washington Post,* December 20: A1, A6.

Schlozman, Kay Lehman and Tierney, John T. 1986. *Organized Interests and American Democracy.* New York: Harper & Row.

Smith, Stephen. 1984. A Computer for Chartridge. *PC Magazine* (3 April): 247–250.

Stevens, William K. 1988. Condominium Owners Grapple With Governing Themselves. *New York Times,* September 1: A18.

Stewart, William E. 1988. *Personnel Law for Community Associations Practitioners.* Alexandria, VA: Communities Association Institute.

Swallow, Wendy. 1984. Panel Backs Regulation of Associations. *The Washington Post,* December 1: F1, F9.

Tarlock, A. Dan. 1989. Residential Community Associations and Land Use Controls. In *Residential Community Associations: Private Governments in the Intergovernmental System?* Pp. 75–93. See ACIR.

Thompson, Dennis F. 1970. *The Democratic Citizen.* Cambridge: Cambridge University Press.

Tocqueville, Alxis de. 1840. *Democracy in America.* Edited and Abridged by Richard D. Heffner. 1956. New York: New American Library.

Tyler, Tom R., Jonathan D. Casper and Bonnie Fisher. 1989. Maintaining Allegiance toward Political Authorities: The Role of Prior Attitudes and the Use of Fair Procedures. *American Journal of Political Science* 33:3 (August): 629–652.

Urban Land Institute. 1964. *The Homes Association Handbook.* Washington, DC: Urban Land Institute.

———. 1985. *Financial Management of Condominium and Homeowners' Associations*. Washington, DC: Urban Land Institute.

U.S. Bureau of the Census. 1990. *Statistical Abstract of the United States, 1990*. Washington, DC: U.S. Government Printing Office.

U.S. Department of Housing and Urban Development. 1975. *HUD Condominium /Cooperative Study*. 3 vols. Washington, DC: HUD.

Vesey, Tom. 1983. Gaithersburg Homeowners Unite, Sue Builders. *The Washington Post,* July 17: B1, B5.

Weiss, Marc A., and John W. Watts. 1989. Community Builders and Community Associations: The Role of Real Estate Developers in Private Residential Governance. In *Residential Community Associations: Private Governments in the Intergovernmental System?* Pp. 95–104. See ACIR.

Williamson, Richard S. 1990. *Reagan's Federalism: His Efforts to Decentralize Government.* Lanham, MD: University Press of America.

———. 1986. A New Federalism: Proposals and Achievements of President Reagan's First Three Years. *Publius* 16 (Winter 1986): 11–28.

Williamson S. and R. Adams. 1987. Dispute Resolution in Condominiums: An Exploratory Study of Condominium Owners in the State of Florida. Human Resources Management Center, College of Business Administration, University of North Florida.

Wilson, James Q. 1973. *Political Organizations.* New York: Basic Books.

———. 1979. American Politics: Then and Now. *Commentary* (February): 41. Cited by Timothy Conlan. 1981. Government Unlocked: Political Constraints on Federal Growth Since The 1930s. In *The Condition of Contemporary Federalism: Conflicting Theories and Collapsing Constraints.* ed. David B. Walker. Pp. 111–140. Washington, DC: U.S. Government Printing Office.

Winokur, James L. 1989a. Association-Administered Servitude Regimes: A Private Property Perspective. In *Residential Community Associations: Private Governments in the Intergovernmental System?* Pp. 85–93. See ACIR.

———. 1989b. The Mixed Blessings of Promissory Servitudes: Toward Optimizing Economic Utility, Individual Liberty, and Personal Identity. *Wisconsin Law Review* 1: 1–97.

———. 1990. Reforming Servitude Regimes: Toward Associational Federalism and Community. *Wisconsin Law Review* 2: 537–552.

Wolfe, David B. 1979. *Condominium and Homeowner Associations That Work.* Washington, D.C.: The Urban Land Institute.

Wrightson, Margaret T. 1989. The Road to *South Carolina:* Intergovernmental Tax Immunity and the Constitutional Status of Federalism. *Publius* 19 (Summer 1989): 39–55.

Zigarmi, Patricia. 1989. Different Strokes for Different Folks: A Situational Approach to Managing People. *Common Ground* (May/June): 29–31.

Index

Adams, R., arguments opposing load shedding, 95; RCA tensions, 137
Adversary democracy, defined, 136
Advisory Commission on Intergovernmental Relations (ACIR), 1988 survey, 7, 118, 119, 123; CC&Rs and local government policing powers, 24; circuit breakers (property taxes), 39; dedication of RCA facilities to local governments, 33; deductibility of assessment fees, 30; disclosure of RCA documents, 35, 36, 139; disclosure of RCA fiscal conditions, 36; fairness of local government officials, 119; inequity in service levels, 31; local government fiscal capacity, 75; performance bonds not required, 31; principle of fiscal equivalence, 98; RCA impact on traffic patterns, 32; RCA interaction with local governments, 25; RCA liability issues, 32; RCA litigation, 144; RCA lobbying efforts, 120, 121, 122, 127; RCA membership, 3; RCA origins, 2, 50; RCA political activities, 151; RCA range of assessment fees, 23; RCA size, 20; RCA suffrage rights, 34, 143; RCA types, 17, 18; RCAs and civic virtue, 134; RCAs deserve greater attention, 8; RCAs and privatization, 9, 28, 63; state capacity, 78; tax equity for HOAs, 29; views on public participation, 134
Ahlbrant, Roger, privatization in Scottsdale, Arizona, 83
Animal control officers, reluctance to enter onto RCA property, 32
Art jury, origins, 49
Articles of incorporation, determine assessment fees, 28, 29, 40; defined, 13; determined by board of directors, 23; origins, 44, 54; problems with during the 1970s, 54; impact RCA lobbying efforts, 116, 129
Attorneys' views on RCAs, 154
Avery v. Midland County (1968), 34, 143

Baltimore, Maryland, Roland Park, 44; HOA origins, 44–47; RCA success story, 92
Barfield, Claude E., governmental centralization, 76
Barton, Stephen E., problem of absentee owners, 137; affordable housing argument, 103; disclosure of RCA documents, 35; opposition to RCAs, 40, 150; principle of fiscal equivalence, 98; RCA members' apathy, 154; RCAs and assessment fees, 58; RCA board members training, 95; RCA board of directors' vacancies, 115; RCAs in California, 117, 118; RCAs and consumer choice, 38; RCAs and contracting out, 146; RCA decisions, 10; RCA descriptions, 3; RCA diversity, 57; RCA litigation,

Barton (*Continued*)
25, 35, 97; RCA members' ignorance, 96; RCA member participation rates, 140; RCA members' satisfaction questioned, 97, 146; RCA political activities, 118, 126, 129, 151, 152; RCAs and public offering statements, 38; RCA quorums, 140; RCA lack of records, 59; RCA size, 20; RCA survey, 7; RCA reserve studies needed, 102; RCA tensions, 137, 143
Beer, Samuel, government growth, 65
Bendick, Marc, privatizing fire services, 83
Bennett, James T., privatization arguments, 81, 83
Beyle, Thad, governor's reforms, 78
Blanket mortgage, limits cooperative association numbers, 16
Book's objectives, listed, 10
Boston, Massachusetts, site of first HOA, 44
Bouton, Edward H., developer of Roland Park, 44; HOA origins, 47
Bowman, Ann O'M., state capacity, 78
Bronx, New York, RCA success story, 92
Brooks, Andree, RCAs and civic virtue, 134; RCA members' apathy, 154; RCA quorums, 115
Brown v. Board of Education, Topeka, Kansas (1954/55), regulation of social relations, 68
Buchanan, James, privatization advocate, 79–82
Burns, James MacGregor, government growth, 65
Business judgment rule, 3, 33, 141

CAI News, 104
California, 124; board vacancies, 115; popularity of condominiums, 50; RCA members violate CC&Rs, 97; disclosure of RCA fiscal conditions, 36; harassment of board members, 137; litigation over goldfish, 62; neighborhood civic associations, 107; RCA member participation rates, 139, 140; RCA political activity, 151; RCAs prevalence in, 18; privatization experiences, 82, 95; reserve studies required, 36, 101; typical size of RCAs, 20; RCA survey, 59
California Department of Real Estate, 7
Casper, Jonathan D., legitimacy of authority argument, 133
CC&Rs, attorneys' view, 154, 159; contracting for services, 88; defined, 1, 2; functions, 23; litigation, 147; members expectations, 157; members ignorance of, 35; origins, 42, 45–47; impact on personal liberty, 99; determine suffrage rights, 34; create tensions, 137
Christian Science Monitor, RCA coverage, 61
Cigler, Allan J., free riders, 112; neighborhood civic associations, 110; pluralism, 157
Circuit breakers (property taxes), 39
Citizen access to services, RCAs' role in altering, 32
Civic virtue, 37, 153, 154; defined, 131; and direct democracy, 132–33; RCA survey results, 133–36
Clark, Peter B., neighborhood civic associations, 106
Colella, Cynthia Cates, constitutional provisions affecting federalism, 67; courts' role in federalism issues, 68
Collective goods, defined, 71; free rider problem, 71
Committee of the Proprietors of Louisburg Square, first HOA, 44
Commodification, RCA's impact on the American landscape, 99
Common Ground, ACIR's survey of RCA board presidents, 25
Common pool goods, defined, 71
Community Association Institute (CAI), 1, 26, 104; difficulty in reaching smaller RCAs, 59, 159; membership, 18; origins, 55; RCA assessment fees, 58; RCA management assistance, 58, 59, 159; RCA meeting notice, 144; RCA numbers, 5, 18, 19, 145; RCAs'

political activity, 152; RCA transition period, 159; RCA welcome packets, 139
Community Associations Institute Research Foundation, RCA newsletter uses, 139; RCA participation rates, 140; RCA members' views, 144
Community builders, defined, 47; role in HOA formation, 47
Community Builders' Council, 49
Condominium associations, advantages, 50; characteristics, 12; defined, 16; disclosure of documents, 139; lobbying efforts, 120, 121; members' tensions, 137; numbers, 18, 50, 51; origins, 41; percentage of all RCAs, 124; early problems, 53; suffrage rights, 34, 142
Condominium declaration, defined, 13
Condominium plat, defined, 13
Conlan, Timothy, American political culture, 69; decentralization argument, 77; government growth, 65, 66; Great Society legislation, 69; Reagan's New Federalism, 70
Contracting out services, 37, 80, 88, 146; amounts contracted out, 83; city experiences with, 82–84; defined, 81
Cooling-off period, RCAs and consumer protection, 38
Cooperative associations, characteristics, 12; defined, 16, 17; percent of RCAs, 19, 124
Corona del Mar, California, RCA tensions, 138
Corporate law, applied to RCAs, 33
Country Club District, The (Kansas City), large, complex federal RCA type, 17, 47, 48
Court Bill of 1937, role in fostering government growth, 67
Creaming, example used to oppose privatization, 85
Cronin, Thomas, government growth, 65

Dale, John G., RCA members' apathy, 154; RCA board members' compensation, 14; RCA member participation rate, 140
Data processing and debt collection, often privatized, 83
Dean, Debra L., RCAs and civic virtue, 134; RCAs and local government interaction, 25; RCA political activities, 152; RCA types, 16
Decentralization, 69–71, 132, 133, 150, 151; argument for, 75–81; load shedding, 81–82; privatization experiences, 82–84
Declaration of covenants, defined, 13; where recorded, 14
Deficits, impediment to government growth, 74
Development standards, RCAs' impact on, 32
Diamond, Martin, local governance praised, 133
Diaz, Raymond, fiduciary duty of RCA board members, 33
Dilger, Robert Jay, 1990 survey, 27, 123, 128; constitutional provisions affecting federalism, 67; decentralization arguments, 78; JTPA creaming of applicants, 85; RCAs and civic virtue, 134, 135; RCAs and local government interaction, 157, 159; RCA member satisfaction, 89, 90; RCA political endorsements, 152; RCA services, 146; spill over benefits, 76
Dilorenzo, Thomas J., privatization arguments, 81, 83
Dowden, James C., arguments for RCAs, 150, 158; CAI created, 18; condominium numbers, 51; condominium origins, 41; condominiums' popularity, 51, 52; condominium problems in the 1970s, 53; FHA rules, 52; financial institution's interest in RCAs, 15; PUD origins, 50; RCA assessment fees, 23; RCA bankruptcies, 30, 100, 101; RCAs and civic virtue, 132, 133; RCA covenants defined, 14; RCA descriptions, 3, 16; RCA management problems, 56, 58; RCA member expectations, 156; RCA member ignorance, 139;

Dowden, James C. (*Continued*)
RCA member satisfaction, 89, 90; RCA numbers, 18; RCA transition period to homeowner control, 16; RCA voting privileges, 142, 143; government regulations, 156
Downer, Philip S., legal rule of reasonableness, 34, 142; RCA litigation, 144

Earl of Leicester, first HOA, 41
Easements, typically recorded in the covenants, 14
Elazar, Daniel J., decentralization argument, 77
Ellickson, Robert, argument for RCAs, 131
Entrepreneurs, role in forming neighborhood civic associations, 113

Federal Home Loan Mortgage Corporation, approval of RCA bylaws and CC&Rs, 14
Federal Housing Administration, financial interest in RCAs' success, 15, 48; mortgage insurance and condominium sales, 52
Federal Housing Authority, approval of RCA bylaws and CC&Rs, 14
Federalist Papers, The federalism defended, 77
Federal National Mortgage Association, approval of RCA bylaws and CC&Rs, 14
Fiduciary duty, of RCA board members, 3, 33, 141
First Amendment, 5, 38, 136; applied to neighborhood civic associations, 109
Fisher, Bonnie, legitimacy of authority, 133
Fixler, Philip E., privatization experiences, 83
Florida, 124; condominiums, 50, 52; condominium incorporation required, 141; views of condominium residents, 95; load shedding, 95; RCA numbers, 18; RCA president threatened with a shotgun, 138; RCA tensions, 137
Food stamps, example of a voucher, 81
Fourteenth Amendment, 5, 38, 136, 144

Frazier, Mark, decentralization argument, 150; deductibility of RCA assessment fees, 30; RCAs and contracting out, 89, 131; RCAs and free riders, 114; RCAs and property values, 24, 37; RCA success stories, 92; RCAs and urban blight, 114
Free rider, defined, 71; role in privatization theory, 79; impact on RCAs, 111–15, 144, 154
Friedman, Milton, private sector argument, 74, 75; privatization argument, 79, 80; vouchers, 82
Friedman, Rose, vouchers, 82

Gans, Curtis B., New England town meetings, 132
Garcia v. San Antonio Metropolitan Transit Authority (1985), overturns *NLC v. Usery*, 68; regulation of commerce, 68
Garreau, Joel, argument for RCAs, 131; RCAs and contracting out, 89; RCA quality of life, 11; RCA voting privileges, 143
Glen Oaks Village, RCA success story, 92
Goldfish, RCA litigation, 61
Gordon, Robert J., justification for governmental action, 73
Gramercy Park, first HOA, 43
Greater Boston Area Association of RCA Presidents, RCA lobbying activity, 127
Great Depression, role in fostering government growth, 67
Great Society, legislation, 69
Guilford, CC&R origins, 45–47
Guilford Association, Baltimore's second HOA, 46

Hadley v. Junior College District (1970), 34, 143

Hartz, Louis, American political culture, 65
Harwood, Richard, public attitude toward government, 70
Hatfields and McCoys, reference to RCA tensions, 138
Hawaii, popularity of condominiums, 50
Hawkins, Robert, RCAs deserve greater attention, 8
Hayes, Michael T., pluralism, 157
Heffner, Richard D., local governance praised, 133
Henig, Jeffrey, American political culture, 69; centralization vs. decentralization, argument, 77, 150; local governments and redistributive policies, 75; privatization arguments, 80, 81, 83–85; vouchers, 82; what should we do question, 8, 64; who should decide question, 8, 64
Hickok, Eugene W., courts' role in federalism issues, 68; discussion of Garcia decision, 68
Holland, Charlotte, Redlands school board meeting, 7
Homeland, HOA origins, 45, 46
Homeowners' associations, characteristics, 12; defined, 16; lobbying efforts, 120, 121; origins, 41, 43; percent of RCAs, 124; suffrage rights, 34; tax equity, 29, 42, 43; voting privileges, 142
Homes Association of Country Club District, 17; federal HOA, 48; precedent for enforcing deed restrictions, 48
Hornblower, Margaret, neighborhood civic associations, 109; RCAs and the NIMBY movement, 7, 117; RCA political activities, 105, 116
Housing Act of 1961, affect on condominium sales, 52
Houston, Texas, RCA tax rebates, 29, 102
Howard, A.E. Dick, courts' role in federalism issues, 68; discussion of Garcia decision, 68
Hunter, Lawrence A., courts' role in federalism issues, 68; discussion of Garcia decision, 68
Hyatt, Wayne S., FHA rules, 52; legal rule of reasonableness, 34, 142; RCA litigation, 144

Insider's lobbying strategy, 126
Isaacson, Andrew L., financial institution's role in approving RCA bylaws, 14; RCA covenants defined, 14; RCA fiscal conditions, 36; RCA membership, 3

J.C. Nichols Investment Company, 48
Jackson, Scott F., financial institution's role in approving RCA bylaws, 14
Japan, American governmental growth, 74; Keynesian economic argument, 74
Japanese yen, competition with the American dollar, 70
Jefferson, Thomas, small government quote, 65
Job Training Partnership Act (JTPA), creaming of applicants, 85
Johnson, Lyndon, role in government growth, 69
Judd, Dennis R., neighborhood civic associations and the OEO, 107

Kansas City, Missouri, site of The Country Club District, 17, 47; HOA origins, 47; RCA success story, 92; RCA tax rebates, 29, 102
Katz, Jeffrey L., neighborhood civic associations, 106–8; privatization experiences, 83, 84
Kearney, Richard C., state capacity, 78
Keynesian economic thought, justification for governmental action, 72, 73
Klein, Dianne, RCA litigation, 62; RCA tensions, 138
Kleine, Douglas, principle of fiscal equivalence, 98; RCAs as political incubators, 129, 152
Korngold, Gerald, RCA CC&Rs, 155;

Korngold, Gerald (*Continued*)
RCA litigation, 147; RCA quorums, 147
Krugh, Robert C., RCA lobbying efforts in New Jersey, 127, 153

Laissez faire, role in government growth, 65
Leicester Square, first HOA, 41
Legal rule of reasonableness, impact on RCA internal rules and procedures, 34; applied to RCAs, 142
Liberal tradition, role in restricting government growth, 65
Liens, RCA authority to impose, 14; in CC&Rs, 15
Little League, 129
Load shedding, 9, 87, 146, 148; arguments for, 88; arguments against, 94–96; defined, 8; practical concerns, 100–103; pros and cons, 151
Local government officials, role in approving RCAs, 4; views concerning RCAs, 156
Local government policing powers, compared to RCAs' CC&Rs, 23
Local government taxes, RCA fairness issue, 27, 28–30, 102, 119– 121, 153
Logic of Collective Action, The free riders, 111
London, England, 43; first HOA, 41
Longhini, Gregory, condominium problems, 53; consumer ignorance, 54, 55; RCA assessment fees, 54; RCA bankruptcy, 30, 100; RCAs defined, 12; RCA phasing problems, 55
Loomis, Burdett A., free riders, 112; neighborhood civic associations, 110; pluralism, 157
Los Angeles Times, RCA coverage, 61
Louisburg Square, site of first HOA, 44

Madison, James, checks and balances, 77
Maintenance services, often privatized, 83
Mansbridge, Jane J., New England town meetings, 132; participation rates, 148; unitary vs. adversary democracy, 136
Marchese, John, RCAs and civic virtue, 134; RCAs role in NIMBY movement, 7; RCA political activities, 105, 116
Maryland, 124
Material incentives, free riders, 112
McBee, Kim, RCA board members compensation, 14; RCA member participation rates, 140, 154
McConnell, Campbell R., governmental growth, 73
Metropolitan Washington Council of Governments, RCA members' satisfaction, 52
Miller, Dean J., transition period to homeowner control, 16
Miller, James P., RCA fights, 35; RCA litigation, 62
Minorities, argument against load shedding, 149
Monetarism, 74
Montgomery County, Maryland, RCA tax rebates, 29, 102
Moore, Stephen, privatization experiences, 83
Mosena, David, condominium problems, 53; consumer ignorance, 54, 55; RCA assessment fees, 54; RCA bankruptcy, 30, 100; RCAs defined, 12; RCA phasing problems, 55

National Association of Homebuilders, creates CAI, 18, 55
National Congress for Community Economic Development, neighborhood civic associations, 107
National Labor Relations Board v. Jones and Laughlin Steel Corporation (1937), regulation of economic production, 68
National League of Cities v. Usery (1976), court sides with the states, 68
Neighborhood civic associations, 116; administrative deficiencies, 111; free

rider problem, 105–8, 110, 114; political activities, 108; suburban vs. urban types, 108
Nelson, Robert H., populist argument for privatization, 84; RCAs and contracting out, 83; RCAs and the diversity vs. uniformity argument, 99; RCAs and property values, 37
Neoclassical economic thought, 74
New England, town meetings, 148
New Federalism, Reagan's proposals, 70
New Jersey, 124; RCA letter writing campaign, 127, 153
Newport Beach, California, litigation over a basketball hoop, 61
New York, disclosure of RCA fiscal conditions, 36; RCAs' numbers, 18; undercounted in surveys, 124
New York City, RCA political activities, 104
New York Times, RCA coverage, 61
Nichols, J.C., builds The Country Club District, 47; community builder, 47; chairs the Community Builders' Council, 49
NIMBY (Not in My Back Yard!), 116, 151; neighborhood civic associations, 108; blamed for obstructing progress, 117; RCAs role in, 7
Norcross, Carl, RCA members' expectations, 156; RCA members' satisfaction, 52, 89
Northwood, HOA origins, 45

Oakerson, Ronald J., courts' role in federalism issues, 68; discussion of Garcia decision, 68; private street associations, 93; RCA efficiency, 150
Oates, Wallace, advocates decentralization, 77
Office of Economic Opportunity, neighborhood civic associations, 106
Olmsted, Frederick Law, planned Roland Park, 44
Olson, Mancur, free riders, 111–13
One person, one vote principle, RCA violates, 157, 158, 160
Palos Verdes, California, litigation over goldfish, 61
Peltason, J.W., government growth, 65
Performance bonds, 31
Peterson, Iver, RCA bankruptcy, 100; disclosure of RCA fiscal conditions, 36; limitations on assessment fee increases, 101; targeting service provision, 91
Pierson, John, New England town meetings, 132
Planned unit developments (PUDs), 4, 5; origins, 50
Planning officials, 1973 survey results, 54, 55; approval of bylaws and CC&Rs, 14
Pluralism, 157; RCAs' role in, 128, 161, 162
Police protection, example of collective good, 72; RCA survey, 119
Policing powers, RCAs behave like local governments, 62
Political socialization, RCAs' role in, 5
Poole, Robert W., privatization experiences, 83
Popper, Frank, opposes NIMBY movement, 117
Populists, privatization views, 84, 93
Pragmatic argument, for RCAs, 93, 94
Principle of fiscal equivalence, 39, 97, 98
Private goods, defined, 71
Private street associations, 92
Privatization, arguments against, 84–86; arguments for, 77–84; defined, 76; origins, 82; RCAs' role in, 9, 87–93; theoretical arguments 63–70. *See also* load shedding
Progressives, 98; role in fostering government growth, 66
Property tax deductions, not for RCAs, 29
Proposition 13, role in privatization, 82; neighborhood civic associations, 107
Proxy voting, 2, 13, 115
P.T.A., 129
Public choice theory, impediment to governmental growth, 70

Public sector, historical growth of, 64–73
Purposive incentives, free riders, 112

Racism, RCAs' role in, 98, 151
Rational choice theory, defined, 77
Rational man model, free riders, 111
RCA board members, candidates, 140; criticisms of, 59, 88; functions, 2; harassment by RCA members, 137; monitor local government action, 126; numbers and compensation, 14; political activities, 135; political aspirations, 152; rate RCA service provision, 21–23
RCA members, ignorance, 96, 138; percent who attend local government meetings, 125; participation rates, 156; opinions, 156. *See also* Residential Community Associations, 1990 survey
Reagan, Ronald, constraints on governmental growth, 69
Real estate developers, assessment fees, 54; CC&Rs, 14; condominium problems, 53; phasing, 55; PUD development, 50, 51; create RCAs, 1, 12, 14, 49, 50; determine RCA services, 2; transition period, 15, 16; views concerning RCAs, 155
Real estate mortgagees, role in approving RCA bylaws and CC&Rs, 15
Redlands, California, school board meeting, 6
Reeves, Mavis Mann, governor's reforms, 78; state legislature reforms, 78
Renters, voting privileges, 34, 160
Reserve studies, 36, 102; RCA members' expectations, 157
Residential Community Associations (RCAs), 1990 survey, 19, 21–23, 26, 27, 123–26, 128, 129, 134–36, 146, 152, 157; articles of incorporation, 15; assessment fees, 1, 23, 29; bankruptcy, 30, 100, 101, 156; bylaws, 13, 15; candidates' forum, 127; CC&Rs, 1, 2, 14, 15, 23, 34, 35, 42, 45–47, 88, 99, 100, 137, 147, 154, 155, 157, 159; civic virtue, 37, 131–44, 153; composition, 124; committees and task forces, 14; consumer protection, 35; defined, 1, 2, 12–15, 160; direct lobbying strategy, 126; disclosure of documents, 35, 54, 139, 154; free rider problems, 114, 115; functions, 1, 2, 12–15, 20–26, 57; governance issues, 34; governmental affairs committees, 118; government legitimacy, 133; history, 1, 3, 12, 41–60; impact on pluralism, 157, 158, 162; impact on property tax revenue, 158; argument for incorporation, 101; insurance requirements, 14; internal politics, 143; litigation, 25, 35, 97, 137, 147; load shedding, 94–103, 149; location, 19, 124; management issues, 54, 56, 58; membership meetings, 13; compared to neighborhood civic associations, 115–17; newsletter, 129, 139; newspaper coverage, 61; nonterritorial type defined, 17; notification of meetings, 158; number, 4, 5, 18–20, 49, 51, 56, 59, 62, 145; phasing problems, 55; political activities, 127, 128, 134, 152; political dynamics, 34; political endorsements, 127; impact on property values, 24; impact on personal liberty, 99, 100; principle of fiscal equivalence, 39, 97, 98; privatization, 9, 86–93; pro and con arguments summarized, 36–40; proxy voting, 2, 13; public offering statements, 38; quorums, 13, 115, 140, 147; relationship with local governments, 26, 27, 104–130; reserve studies, 36, 101, 102, 158; services, 1, 21–23, 31, 39, 91, 125; size, 9, 19, 20, 57; social contract, 160; tax equity issues, 28, 102, 103, 120, 121, 127; territorial type defined, 17; three types defined, 16; views of local government officials, 156; views of real estate developers, 155; views of attorneys, 154; voting privileges, 14, 142–44
Reston, Virginia, site of large RCA, 57
Reynolds v. Sims (1964), 34, 143

Riendeau, Albert, quote on RCA living, 11
Roland Park, CC&R origins, 45, 46; HOA origins, 44, 47, 48
Roland Park Company, CC&R origins, 45; HOA origins, 44, 46
Roland Park Roads and Maintenance Corporation, Baltimore's first HOA, 46
Roosevelt, Franklin, role in fostering government growth, 67
Rosenberry, Katharine, fiduciary duty of RCA board members, 3, 33; legal standards applied to RCAs, 3, 141; RCAs and contracting out, 88
Ruggles, Samuel, HOA origins, 43
Rural/Metro Fire Protection Company, privatizing fire services, 83

St. Louis, Missouri, RCA success story, 92
St. Louis County, Missouri, private street associations, 92
Salamon, Lester, impediments to government growth, 70
Salisbury, Robert H., free riders, 113; neighborhood civic associations, 106
Savas, E.S., defines types of goods, 71; on government growth, 72; on the private sector, 73; privatization, 63, 80, 83, 84; remedy for free riders and collective goods, 72
Schlozman, Kay Lehman, free riders, 111, 113; insider's lobbying strategy, 127; pluralism limitations, 161
Scottsdale, Arizona, privatizing fire services, 83
Segal, Earl L., covenants defined, 14; disclosure of RCA fiscal conditions, 36; financial institution's role in approving RCA bylaws, 14; RCA membership, 3
Segregation of land uses, by RCAs, 24
Selective benefits, free riders, 112
Seniority system, impediment to governmental growth, 69
Servitudes, duration, 155; when enforceable, 155; legal implications, 154
Silverman, Carol, problem of absentee owners, 137; affordable housing argument, 103; disclosure of RCA documents, 35; opposition to RCAs, 40, 150; principle of fiscal equivalence, 98; RCA members' apathy, 154; RCAs and assessment fees, 58; RCA board members training, 95; RCA board of directors' vacancies, 115; RCAs in California, 117, 118; RCAs and consumer choice, 38; RCAs and contracting out, 146; RCA decisions, 10; RCA descriptions, 3; RCA diversity, 57; RCA litigation, 25, 35, 97; RCA members' ignorance, 96; RCA member participation rates, 140; RCA members' satisfaction questioned, 97, 146; RCA political activities, 118, 126, 129, 151, 152; RCAs and public offering statements, 38; RCA quorums, 140; RCA lack of records, 59; RCA size, 20; RCA survey, 7; RCA reserve studies needed, 102; RCA tensions, 137, 143
Smith, Adam, role in privatization theory, 79
Social contract, defined, 160
Social scientists, view of RCAs, 157
Solidary incentives, free riders, 112
South Carolina v. Baker (1988), general welfare clause, 68
South Dakota v. Dole (1987), general welfare clause, 68
Spill over benefits, justification for centralization, 76
Spillovers, 81
Spyglass Homeowners' Association, RCA tensions, 138
Stanford University Law School, 131
Starr, Paul, opposition to privatization, 85, 86
State courts, 3
Steward Machine Company v. Davis (1937), general welfare clause, 68
Supply side economics, 74

Tarlock, Dan, RCA definition, 3; RCA functions, 2

Tax rebates, 28, 29, 102, 103, 120, 121, 127, 153
Tenth Amendment, used in *National League of Cities v. Usery*, 68; states' rights, 67
Territorial RCAs, 26
Texas, 124; RCAs prevalence in, 18
Thompson, Dennis F., prospects for participatory democracy, 132; views on participation, 134
Tierney, John T., free riders, 111, 113; insider's lobbying strategy, 127; pluralism's limitations, 161
Tocqueville, Alexis de, local governance praised, 133, 150
Toll goods, defined, 71
Trash collection, 1, 2, 9, 20, 21, 23, 27, 28, 32, 86, 126; privatization experiences, 82, 83; tax equity, 102
Tullock, Gordon, privatization advocate, 79, 80, 82
Tulsa, O lahoma, RCA success story, 92
Tyler, Tom R., legitimacy of authority, 133

U.S. Bureau of the Census, condominium numbers, 51
U.S. Constitution, federalism provisions, 67; RCAs infringe on members' rights, 136
U.S. Department of Housing and Urban Development, RCA members' ignorance, 35; RCA members' satisfaction, 52
U.S. Supreme Court, role in determining federalism issues, 67; role in fostering government growth, 67, 68
Unit deeds, defined, 13
Unitary democracy, defined, 136
University of Michigan's Institute for Social Research, public's attitude toward government, 70
Urban Land Institute, blanket mortgages, 17; role in creating CAI 18, 55; CC&R origins, 45; forms the Community Builders' Council, 49; condominium numbers, 51; Country Club District in Kansas City, 17, 48; favors RCAs, 37; financial institution's interest in RCAs, 14, 15; RCA member satisfaction, 89; research on HOAs, 41, 44, 46, 47

Vehicle towing and storage, often privatized, 83
Vesey, Tom, RCAs' role in the NIMBY movement, 7; RCA political activities, 105, 116
Veteran's Administration, approval of RCA bylaws and CC&Rs, 14; RCA financing, 52
Virginia, 124; disclosure of RCA fiscal conditions, 36
Vouchers, 80; defined, 81

Walker, David B., Reagan's New federalism, 70
Wall Street Journal, RCA coverage, 61
Washington, D.C., RCAs' prevalence in, 18
Washington Metropolitan Council of Governments, RCA member satisfaction, 61, 90
Washington Post, RCA coverage, 61
Waterman Place Association, RCA success story, 92
Watts, John W., CAI origins, 56; the Community Builders' Council, 42, 47, 49; court enforcement of CC&Rs, 43; emphasis on costs, 57; precedents for enforcing deed restrictions, 48; RCA functions during the 1970s, 52; RCA growth, 57; RCA management problems, 58
Weiss, Marc A., CAI origins, 56; the Community Builders' Council, 42, 47, 49; court enforcement of CC&Rs, 43; emphasis on costs, 57; precedents for enforcing deed restrictions, 48; RCA functions during the 1970s, 52; RCA growth, 57; RCA management problems, 58
What should we do question, explanation, 63, 64; justification for studying RCAs, 8

Who should decide question, explanation, 63, 64; justification for studying RCAs, 8
Wild animals, example of a common pool good, 71
Williamson, Richard S., decentralization argument, 77, 78; Reagan's New Federalism, 70
Williamson, S., argument opposing load shedding, 95; RCA tensions, 137
Wilson, James Q., free riders, 112, 113; comment on governmental activism, 69; neighborhood civic associations, 106
Winokur, James L., arguments against RCAs, 150; duration of CC&Rs, 155; disclosure of RCA documents, 35, 36; RCAs and consumer choice, 38; RCAs and consumer protection, 38; RCA litigation, 25, 97, 147; RCA members' discontent, 138, 146; RCA members' knowledge of CC&Rs, 35, 96; RCA number, 5; RCAs' impact on personal liberties, 99, 100; RCAs' impact on property values, 39; segregation of land uses, 24
Wrightson, Margaret T., courts' role in federalism issues, 68